LEVI LUSKO

WITH TAMA FORTNER

ROAR

LIKE A LION

90 DEVOTIONS TO A COURAGEOUS FAITH

ILLUSTRATED BY CATHERINE PEARSON

An Imprint of Thomas Nelson

Published in Nashville, Tennessee, by Tommy Nelson. Tommy Nelson is an imprint of Thomas Nelson. Thomas Nelson is a registered trademark of HarperCollins Christian Publishing, Inc.

Published in association with the literary agency of Wolgemuth & Associates.

Tama Fortner is represented by Cyle Young of C.Y.L.E. (Cyle Young Literary Elite, LLC), a literary agency.

Tommy Nelson titles may be purchased in bulk for educational, business, fund-raising, or sales promotional use. For information, please email SpecialMarkets@ThomasNelson.com.

Scripture quotations marked ESV are taken from the ESV® Bible (The Holy Bible, English Standard Version®). Copyright © 2001 by Crossway, a publishing ministry of Good News Publishers. Used by permission. All rights reserved. Scripture quotations marked ICB are taken from the International Children's Bible®. Copyright © 1986, 1988, 1999, 2015 by Thomas Nelson. Used by permission. All rights reserved. Scripture quotations marked NCV are taken from the New Century Version®. Copyright © 2005 by Thomas Nelson. Used by permission. All rights reserved. Scripture quotations marked NIV are taken from the Holy Bible, New International Version®, NIV®. Copyright © 1973, 1978, 1984, 2011 by Biblica, Inc.® Used by permission of Zondervan. All rights reserved worldwide. www.zondervan.com. The "NIV" and "New International Version" are trademarks registered in the United States Patent and Trademark Office by Biblica, Inc.® Scripture quotations marked NLT are taken from the Holy Bible, New Living Translation. Copyright © 1996, 2004, 2015 by Tyndale House Foundation. Used by permission of Tyndale House Ministries, Carol Stream, Illinois 60188. All rights reserved.

ISBN 978-1-4002-2556-9 (audiobook)
ISBN 978-1-4002-2433-3 (eBook)
ISBN 978-1-4002-2436-4 (HC)

Library of Congress Cataloging-in-Publication Data

Names: Lusko, Levi, author. | Fortner, Tama, 1969- author. | Pearson, Catherine, illustrator.
Title: Roar like a lion : 90 devotions to a courageous faith / Levi Lusko with Tama Fortner ; illustrated by Catherine Pearson.
Description: Nashville, Tennessee, USA : Thomas Nelson, [2021] | Audience: Ages 6-10 | Summary: "Popular author and pastor Levi Lusko brings key ideas from his bestselling book Through the Eyes of a Lion into these motivating devotions for kids, encouraging them to move toward their everyday challenges with powerful, God-inspired bravery"-- Provided by publisher.
Identifiers: LCCN 2021011606 (print) | LCCN 2021011607 (ebook) | ISBN 9781400224364 (hardcover) | ISBN 9781400224333 (epub)
Subjects: LCSH: Children--Prayers and devotions--Juvenile literature. | Courage--Prayers and devotions--Juvenile literature.
Classification: LCC BV265 .L87 2021 (print) | LCC BV265 (ebook) | DDC 242/.62--dc23
LC record available at https://lccn.loc.gov/2021011606
LC ebook record available at https://lccn.loc.gov/2021011607

Written by Levi Lusko with Tama Fortner
Illustrated by Catherine Pearson

Printed in Korea

22 23 24 25 SAM 6 5 4 3

Mfr: SAM / Seoul, Korea / February 2022 / PO #12135965

For Lenya Avery Lusko, aka Lenya Lion.
Thank you for teaching me how to roar.
I miss you fiercely and can't wait
to see you in heaven!

CONTENTS

INTRODUCTION

I **LOVE LIONS. THEY'RE FIERCE,** regal, and strong—and just incredibly amazing. So when Jesus is called the Lion of the tribe of Judah, it's a *huge* compliment!

Not too long ago, I went on a mini safari in South Africa where I learned all kinds of cool things about lions. Did you know that adult lions are *apex predators*? That means they're at the top of the food chain. No other animals mess with or hunt an apex predator! Lions also stick together. They're the only members of the cat family that live in groups, called *prides*. These prides can have as many as fifteen or more lions, all working together to hunt and raise their young.

The way lions hunt is really cool too. They're the only cats with tasseled tails, and they use them to "talk" to other lions while they're out on a hunt. Lions also walk on their tiptoes, kind of like a ballerina or a boxer! This makes them light on their feet, helping an adult lion run up to fifty miles an hour. (That's as fast as a car!) And they can jump as much as thirty-six feet in a single bound. (Imagine laying a wooden telephone pole on the ground and jumping from one end to the other—that's what lions can do!) A lion's eyesight is six times better than ours, especially in the dark. It's like they're wearing night-vision binoculars all the time.

Lions don't start out super-tough and strong. When it's born, a lion cub is completely blind and has to stay close to its parents and the pride for protection. In fact, lion cubs spend the first two years of their lives growing and learning all they need to know to survive in the wild.

Just like a lion cub, you'll spend the first few years of your life growing and learning the things you need to know to survive in this wild world. One of the reasons I wrote *Roar Like a Lion* was to help you do just that.

There are ninety devotions in this book. Each starts off with a Bible verse—what could be better? Then there's a devotion about God and how amazing He is. In "Did You Know?" you'll learn super-cool stuff from history (my favorite subject!). And in "Get Ready to Roar!" I'll be giving you a few missions to build up your courage and your "roar" in this world. Each day's devotion finishes up with a prayer to connect your heart to God.

Roar Like a Lion was written in honor of my daughter Lenya. She lives with Jesus now, but she roared through this life like an amazing little lion—just like I know she's roaring through heaven now. Lenya was curious about everything, and I hope that *Roar Like a Lion* will jump-start your curiosity and encourage you to dig deeper into God's Word.

My prayer is that as you journey through this book—whether at bedtime, during a meal, or even as a part of your school lesson—*Roar Like a Lion* will anchor your heart to heaven and grow your love for Jesus, the real lion King!

—Levi

P.S. Speaking of anchors, be on the lookout! Anchors are hidden all throughout the illustrations in this book. Why? Because anchors are one of the coolest pictures of what it looks like to have Jesus as your Savior and Friend. (Check out "The Anchor" on page 134 to find out why.) There are twenty anchors in all. How many can you find? The answers are on page 192.

1

ROAR LIKE A LION

God did not give us a spirit that makes us afraid. He gave us a spirit of power and love and self-control.

2 TIMOTHY 1:7 ICB

HAVE YOU HEARD THE saying "as brave as a lion"? We compare being brave to being like a lion because, well, lions aren't really afraid of much. Not buffalos, rhinos, elephants, or even crocodiles. They weigh up to five hundred pounds, which is like fifty house cats in one big pile. Together, their weight, strength, and fearlessness make them one powerful force in the wild.

The Bible says, "Good people are as brave as a lion" (Proverbs 28:1 ICB).

They have the courage to do what God says is good and right. Even if everyone else is doing wrong. Their lives "roar" with the goodness of God.

Now, if you've ever heard a lion roar—whether at the zoo or in a movie—you know it's a sound so big and loud that everyone stops and takes notice. And that's exactly what God wants your life to do. He wants it to roar so loud that everyone stops and takes notice.

How can your life roar? Well, it has nothing to do with your vocal cords and everything to do with daring to live differently from the rest of the world. Your life roars when you have the courage to follow God no matter what. Being "as brave as a lion" doesn't mean you're never afraid. But it *does* mean you choose to do the good and right thing anyway. That kind of courage doesn't come from inside you or from your own strength. It can only come from the Spirit and power of God.

So go ahead and roar like a lion. Let the whole world know how awesome and amazing and powerful your God is!

LORD, HELP ME ROAR LIKE A LION SO THAT I CAN TELL THE WHOLE WORLD ABOUT YOU. AMEN.

DID YOU KNOW?

In the wild, lions roar for three reasons: to let other lions know where they are, to show how powerful they are, and to scare off an enemy. Your life should roar for the same reasons: to let other believers know where you are and that they aren't alone, to show how powerful God is, and to scare off your enemy, the devil. Because when you roar with the power of God, the devil runs away (James 4:7).

2

SO YOU WANT TO BE BRAVE

On the day I called to you, you answered me. You made me strong and brave.

PSALM 138:3 NCV

SO YOU WANT TO be brave. You want to stand up for what's right, help the hopeless, and fight evil. You want to shine the light of God's love and truth into this dark world. You want to fly through the air and swoop down to rescue someone in the nick of time. Okay, maybe not that last one. (But wouldn't that be *so* cool?) To do those things, you need to be brave. Well, here's what you need to know about being brave: You don't need muscles like Superman or lightning-fast reflexes like Wonder

Woman. You don't need to climb walls like Spider-Man or talk to dolphins like Aquaman. You don't need Captain America's shield or Iron Man's iron suit. (But again, wouldn't that be *so* cool?) Truth is, there's only one thing you need to be brave.

God.

Because God has *all* the superpowers. He soars on the wind to rescue His people (Psalm 18:10). He commands the thunder and the lightning (Psalm 18:14). No enemy can stand up to Him! And when you believe He is who He says He is and that He'll do what He says He'll do—when you love, trust, and obey Him—God will pour His power into you (Ephesians 1:19–20). He will help you be brave enough to do what is right. And *that's* what makes a real superhero.

DID YOU KNOW?

The super-est superheroes aren't found in movies or comic books. They're the real-life ones, like Harriet Tubman. Harriet was born a slave in Maryland sometime around 1820. She was beaten, and often she was fed only scraps. In 1849, Harriet used the Underground Railroad—a network of people who hid slaves trying to escape—to get to Pennsylvania and to freedom. But that wasn't enough for Harriet. She became a conductor on the Underground Railroad and helped more than three hundred slaves escape. Harriet became known as "Moses" because, like Moses in the Bible, she led her people to freedom.

LORD, I WANT TO BE BRAVE—NOT SO THAT I CAN BE LIKE A SUPERHERO BUT SO I CAN TELL THE WORLD HOW SUPER-AMAZING YOU ARE. AMEN.

3

YOU DO YOU?

Do what is right to other people. Love being kind to others. And live humbly, trusting your God.

MICAH 6:8 ICB

HAVE YOU HEARD THE saying "You do you"? It's pretty popular these days. It means you should do your own thing—whatever makes you happy. Of course, that also means that everyone else should be free to do their own thing—whatever makes them happy. Sounds good, right? What if the thing that makes you happy makes someone else unhappy? Or whatever makes someone else happy leaves you feeling hurt? That definitely doesn't sound so good. God has a much better plan. Instead of *you do you*, God says you should *do what's right for others*.

What does that mean? An awesome verse in the little book of Micah sums it up for us: "Do what is right to other people. Love being kind to others. And live humbly, trusting your God" (6:8 ICB). Because, as it turns out, living the way God wants you to isn't about *you* at all. It's about God, and it's about others. You see, God created you to show everyone around you how amazing and full of love He is. The best way to do that is to treat everyone the way God treats you—with lots of love and kindness.

So instead of ignoring your brother, let him play the video game with you. Instead of interrupting your friends to talk about what *you* want to talk about, listen and show interest in what they care about. Help your dad put away the groceries, and offer to help your mom make dinner.

Get out there and show the world how awesome God really is!

GET READY TO ROAR!

Micah 6:8 gives us three ways to live for God. Today, let's work on kindness. Who can you be extra-kind to today? Maybe include your little brother or sister in a game with your friends, or let them ride in the best seat in the car—even if you already called it. Offer to bring in the mail for an older neighbor. Or be kind to your community by picking up litter. How many kind things can you do today?

LORD, TEACH ME TO BE WHO YOU CREATED ME TO BE SO I CAN DO WHAT IS RIGHT, BE KIND, AND TRUST IN YOU. AMEN.

4

SCARED AND BRAVE

The LORD your God will go ahead of you and fight for you.

DEUTERONOMY 1:30 NCV

WHEN IT COMES TO trouble, a lot of times you can avoid it by making good choices. For example, if you tell the truth, you won't get in trouble for lying. If you keep your eyes on your own test, no one will think you're a cheat. If you are kind and helpful, you won't get in trouble for being a jerk.

But there are some kinds of trouble we can't avoid, no matter how good our choices are. Things like getting sick, hearing our parents fighting, or losing someone we love. Nobody chooses for those kinds of things to happen, but sometimes, well, they just do.

When trouble comes, it can be scary. And it's okay to be scared. But you don't have to be stuck feeling afraid. You can be scared *and* brave at the same time. How? By calling out to God in prayer. He's never scared, and He's always ready to help.

God starts answering your prayers even before you finish praying (Isaiah 65:24). And He never leaves you to fight your way through a jungle of troubles on your own. God doesn't just fight by your side either. No, He goes ahead of you and starts fighting *for* you. He clears the way and makes sure you have everything you need to get through to the other side.

The next time trouble finds you, call out to God—and then watch to see how He answers you.

DID YOU KNOW?

Corrie ten Boom was working in her family's watch shop when the Nazis invaded Holland. The Nazis began rounding up Jews and sending them to concentration camps where millions of people died. Corrie wasn't Jewish, so she could have ignored what was happening around her. Instead, she bravely risked her life by hiding Jewish people in a secret room in her house. When the Nazis found out, she and her family were arrested and taken to a camp. She survived, and later—with God's help—she was even able to forgive those who hurt her in the camp.

GOD, THANK YOU FOR ALWAYS HEARING AND ANSWERING ME. I TRUST YOU TO ALWAYS FIGHT FOR ME. AMEN.

5

WANNABE LION

Stay alert! Watch out for your great enemy, the devil. He prowls around like a roaring lion, looking for someone to devour.

1 PETER 5:8 NLT

THE LION CROUCHES IN the grass, not moving a muscle or making a sound. He's watching his prey—the prey that doesn't even know the enemy is there. And he's waiting, just waiting for the perfect moment to . . . *pounce!*

It's easy to see how dangerous a lion is when he's stalking his prey, but the devil is even more dangerous. The Bible says he's like a lion—crouching and hiding, prowling around, waiting for the perfect moment to pounce! Now, the devil doesn't want to munch on your legs or toes. Instead, he wants to eat up your peace, joy, and trust in God. Those are his favorite snacks.

But the devil is only *like* a lion. He's a wannabe who wishes he could be as powerful as the real Lion. It's like he's roaring from inside a lion costume.

Who's the real Lion? Jesus, the Lion of Judah! When you trust Jesus and believe He's God's own Son, He comes to stand between you and the devil. And no wannabe lion can get past Him.

In the wild, you can spot a lion by looking for animals that are upset, worried, and scared. That's a pretty good way to spot the devil too. If you're upset, worried, or scared, ask God to show you what lies the devil might be roaring at you. Then take a look at what the Bible says is true. Like the fact that not even a wannabe lion can take away God's love and care for you (Romans 8:38–39).

DID YOU KNOW?

Why is Jesus called "the Lion of Judah"? Well, the lion is the "king of all beasts," while Jesus is the "King of all kings." That's why Jesus is sometimes compared to a lion. The Judah part comes from a guy named Judah. He was one of Jacob's twelve sons (Genesis 49). Judah was also the great-great-great-*whole bunch of greats*-granddad of Jesus, which makes Jesus from the family of Judah. That's why Jesus is called the Lion of Judah. And when He roars, that wannabe lion named Satan runs away like a scaredy-cat!

LORD, WHEN THE DEVIL ROARS AT ME, HELP ME REMEMBER THAT YOU ARE BIGGER AND STRONGER THAN HE COULD EVER BE! AMEN.

6

NOT THE END

Jesus said to her, "I am the resurrection and the life. The one who believes in me will live, even though they die."

JOHN 11:25 NIV

WHEN SOMEONE WE LOVE dies, it's often called "losing someone." I guess that's because we've lost the gift of spending more time with that person. What's left behind is this big, ugly hole of emptiness where there used to be hugs and smiles and laughter. And it hurts. Boy, does it hurt. It's hard to get up and keep going. Sometimes it takes every scrap of courage we have just to face the everyday stuff of life.

But I've got to tell you something that's so important: *losing someone you love isn't the end of the story.* It's just a curve in the road. When we love and trust God, death is just the beginning— the beginning of a whole new life in heaven that's more wonderful and more real than anything we could ever imagine. That person you love is singing, dancing, and loving their new life with Jesus. And one day, you'll be with them again—singing, dancing, and loving your new life with Jesus too.

Until then, yeah, there's going to be some sad times and some tears. But it *will* get easier. And you need to know that it's okay to be happy again. You can still show love and honor to the person you lost by dancing, laughing, and remembering all the wonderful things about that person. And if you need to cry, that's okay too.

One day, all our hurt will end forever, and we'll find the ones we lost waiting for us in heaven.

GET READY TO ROAR!

When you lose someone you love, the hurt can be so huge that it blocks out everything else. Ask God to fill your thoughts with good and special memories of that person—all the things that make you smile. That might happen a little bit at a time, so start a collection. Write them in a journal and paste in favorite pictures to remind you of times you shared together. And when the hurt gets huge, look back through your collection, remember the happy times, and know that it's okay to smile.

LORD, EVEN WHEN I AM HURTING, I PRAISE YOU BECAUSE DEATH ISN'T THE END, AND I'LL SEE MY SPECIAL PERSON AGAIN. AMEN.

7

JUST PASSING THROUGH

"There are many rooms in my Father's house. . . .
I am going there to prepare a place for you."

JOHN 14:2 NCV

TEMPORARY. IT MEANS THAT something will last only for a time. That's what life here on earth is: temporary. We're just passing through. If you're a follower of Jesus, that's actually very good news. Because you're just passing through on your way to heaven—a place so wonderful that words can't describe it. And here's some even better news: You're not just headed for heaven. You're headed for a place that Jesus has prepared *just for you*. He's painted and polished and put your name on the door.

Why is that important? Because when you're up against a problem—whether it's a little one or a mountain-size one—you can know it's only temporary too. Knowing there will be an end to that problem can give you the courage to keep getting up and facing it.

So if you are struggling with something—your best friend moved away, you or someone you love is sick, or your parents are splitting up—don't let the hugeness of that problem stop you in your tracks. This life is like a journey, and trouble is just a part of that journey. But you're passing through on the way to someplace wonderful. Keep putting one foot in front of the other. Keep doing the next thing you know is right, and then the next. Sure, it takes courage. But you can do this. Because God is on your side, and you're just passing through.

DID YOU KNOW?

Everything on earth is temporary. Just ask the dinosaurs! Dinosaurs may be extinct, but we know a lot about them. How? People have found the fossils of their bones. Dinosaur bones were first found back in the 1820s by Dr. Gideon Mantell. But it was Dr. Richard Owen who gave dinosaurs their name, calling them *Dinosauria*, which means "terrible lizard."

GOD, WHEN TROUBLES SEEM LIKE THEY'LL NEVER GO AWAY, HELP ME REMEMBER THAT I'M JUST PASSING THROUGH. AMEN.

WHO MADE IT POSSIBLE?

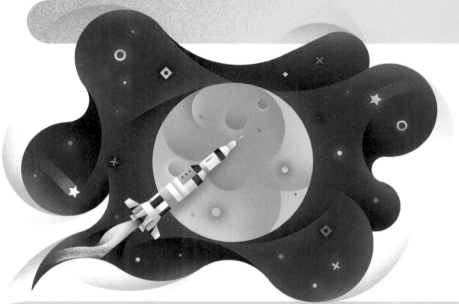

We have many people of faith around us.
Their lives tell us what faith means.

HEBREWS 12:1 ICB

WHEN ASTRONAUT NEIL ARMSTRONG climbed aboard the *Apollo 11* in July of 1969, he carried some historical treasures with him. They were pieces of the propeller and fabric from the wing of the *Wright Flyer*—the plane flown by Orville and Wilbur Wright in the world's first powered flight back in 1903. Armstrong then went on to make history himself as the first man to step foot on the moon.

Why did Armstrong carry those things all the way into space with him? He was a huge admirer of the Wright brothers and had read what they wrote about flying. But more than that, the Wright brothers were the pioneers of *aviation* (or flying). In many ways, it was their study, research, and inventions that led to the flight to the moon. Armstrong's 240,000-mile flight to the moon wouldn't have been possible without the Wright brothers' baby step of a 120-foot long, 12-second flight. Armstrong wanted to remember and honor them.

Who made believing in God possible for you? Who showed you the love and goodness of God? Did you grow up in a family surrounded by people who loved God? Or was it a friend, a teacher, or even a book that pointed you to Him? Say a prayer of thanks to God for them—and thank them in person, if you can. Then remember and honor what they did for you by showing someone else the love and goodness of God. And who knows? Maybe someday, someone will be thanking *you* for showing them the way to God.

GOD, THANK YOU FOR THOSE WHO HAVE SHOWN ME HOW GOOD YOU ARE. LET ME LIVE IN A WAY THAT SHOWS OTHERS HOW TO FIND YOU. AMEN.

9

HAPPY TIMES ARE COMING

Crying may last for a night. But joy comes in the morning.

PSALM 30:5 ICB

IMAGINE A STORM SO dark and fierce that you can't see your hand in front of your face—not even in the middle of the day! That's what happened one Sunday in 1935. But that storm wasn't made of rain, sleet, or snow. It was made of dust!

Back in the 1930s, a terrible drought hit parts of the United States and lasted for *years*. It was especially bad in the Midwest, where the promise of free land had brought thousands of "suitcase farmers" to the flat prairies. They ripped up millions of acres of prairie grass to plant wheat—not knowing the grass kept the soil healthy. When the drought hit, the wheat died, and the land became a desert known as the Dust Bowl. Winds whipped up huge dust storms called "black blizzards." One of the worst happened on April 14, 1935—a day known as Black Sunday. Walls of dust two thousand feet tall and two hundred miles wide covered cities from Colorado to Texas. People hid in cars, in basements, and under beds. Over three hundred thousand tons of dust were carried away by that storm—some landing over a thousand miles away!

Those people probably thought the Dust Bowl years would last forever. But they didn't. President Franklin D. Roosevelt had millions of trees planted to block the winds. Rains fell, farmers learned better ways to farm, and the prairies were beautiful again.

In this life, you're going to have dark times—a move, a loss, a sickness, or just a really bad day. But those hard times won't last forever. That's God's promise. Keep praying and keep trusting God. Happy times are coming!

DID YOU KNOW?

The Sahara is a huge desert in Africa, but imagine seeing part of it in your own backyard! It happens every year. Winds pick up millions of tons of dust and blow it across the Atlantic Ocean, all the way to the Amazon rain forest, where it fertilizes the soil. As that dust passes by the US, the eastern part of the country gets quite a show—those dust particles cause some spectacular sunsets. It's a desert in the sky!

FATHER, NO MATTER HOW HARD THINGS GET, I'LL TRUST YOU TO HELP ME FIND HAPPY TIMES AGAIN. AMEN.

10

IN THE NEWS

Jesus said to them, "My Father never stops working, and so I keep working, too."

JOHN 5:17 NCV

AN EARTHQUAKE SHOOK THE *city! A bomb exploded! Armed robbers escaped!*

Sounds like something from the latest action movie, doesn't it? But it could just as easily be the headlines you see trending online. There's some pretty scary stuff in this world!

King Solomon, who was the wisest man who ever lived (except Jesus, of course!), once said, "There is nothing new under the sun" (Ecclesiastes 1:9 ESV). And he was right. Ever since Adam and Eve first nibbled on that forbidden fruit, bad things have been happening in this world—it's nothing new.

But even before Adam and Eve tasted that fruit, *God* had been happening in this world. He is *always* here, and He is *always* working in the lives of His people.

Yes, bad things happen in this world, and those bad things are so easy to see. But good things happen too. Search for the ways God is working in everything that happens. When people are sick and hurting, He is there, working through the hands of the doctors and nurses. When there's danger or an accident, He's there in the courage of helpful neighbors, strong firefighters and police, and tough soldiers.

And you know what? God wants to work through *you*! What helpful thing is God asking you to do? It can be as big as standing up to a bully or as simple as hugging a friend when he has a bad day. Be brave, and let God show His goodness through you.

GET READY TO ROAR!

We hear enough bad news. Why not share some of your good news? What goodness do you see in this world? Where do you see God working? Use that good news to create your own newspaper story. Make up a headline and draw a picture to match. You could even write up a whole story. Share it with your family, neighbors, or friends. Because everyone could use some good news!

DEAR GOD, IT'S SO EASY TO SEE ALL THE BAD THINGS HAPPENING. PLEASE SHOW ME YOUR GOODNESS AND ALL THE WAYS YOU ARE WORKING IN THIS WORLD. AND HELP ME BRING SOME GOODNESS TO THE WORLD TOO. AMEN.

COURAGE IN THE DARK

My God brightens the darkness around me.

PSALM 18:28 ICB

THERE'S SOMETHING ABOUT THE dark that makes everything bigger and scarier. Turn out the light, and the chair in the corner suddenly becomes a monster waiting to pounce. Those curtains swaying in the breeze of the ceiling fan must be hiding something terrible. And that *creeeak* from the hallway just can't be good. It can take every bit of courage you have to jump up and turn on the light—or shout for Mom or Dad!

Fear and darkness don't just come around at night, though. Fear can trip us up right in the middle of the day. The friend you thought was always in your corner starts a monster-size rumor, and suddenly everyone's laughing at you. Your rock-solid home sways like curtains in the wind when your parents have a fight. The shot you have to get at your doctor's appointment looks like it will be really painful. And that creak of worry you hear inside your mind says things just can't be good. That's when it's time to gather up every bit of courage and shout out to God. He'll hear you every time (Psalm 55:16–17).

Tell Him about the friend who turned out not to be a friend, about your parents' fight, and about the worries whirling through your head. He'll shine the light of His love on those dark fears and help you figure out just what to say and do. And He'll walk right beside you the whole way (Psalm 23:4). Whenever darkness creeps into your world, shout out to God—and He'll chase the darkness away!

DID YOU KNOW?

Owls have eyes like binoculars. Seriously! While human eyes are shaped like spheres, an owl's eyes are shaped like long tubes. These tubes act much like binoculars and help them spot prey from yards away, even in the darkness. Because owls are most active at night, they are called *nocturnal*, which means they sleep during the day and are awake at night. And since they can see so well at night, they're never scared of the dark!

LORD, BECAUSE YOU ARE WITH ME, I CAN BE BRAVE. YOUR LOVE IS BRIGHT ENOUGH TO CHASE AWAY THE DARKNESS OF FEAR. AMEN.

12

BUT GOD . . .

> **"For people this is impossible, but for
> God all things are possible."**
>
> MATTHEW 19:26 NCV

TWO OF THE BEST words you'll ever hear are "but God." Why? Because we can get ourselves into all kinds of sticky messes and impossible situations. *But God* can do impossible things—and He often does to save His people. Just think about it:

- Daniel's enemies had him thrown into a lions' den. *But God* sent His angel to shut the lions' mouths to keep Daniel safe (Daniel 6).
- Joseph's brothers were so jealous of him that they sold him to be a slave in Egypt. *But God* used their evil plans to save the lives of many people, including Joseph's brothers (Genesis 50:20).

- Joshua stared up at the mighty, impossible-to-tear-down walls of Jericho and wondered what to do. *But God* gave him an unusual battle plan that sent those walls tumbling down with a stroll, a trumpet blast, and a shout (Joshua 6).

Hungry lions, evil plans, a mighty wall? Impossible! But God did the impossible.

The greatest example of "but God" is the one that He offers to each of us. You see, we mess up and sin all the time. Every single one of us. Sometimes by accident, and sometimes on purpose. That sin makes it impossible for us to be with Him. *But God* sent Jesus to take away our sins so that we could be close to God again (Romans 6:23).

Forgiveness for sins and life in heaven forever? Sounds impossible! But God made the impossible possible.

DID YOU KNOW?

An *archaeologist* (ar-kee-OL-uh-jist) is someone who studies the objects of the past to learn more about what happened. Archaeologists have studied the ancient ruins of Jericho, and they have found proof that Jericho's walls fell just as the Bible says they did, falling on top of themselves. They even found a section of the wall that didn't fall. This might be where Rahab lived. Rahab was the woman the Israelite spies promised to save, and her house stood against the wall (Joshua 2, 6).

HEAVENLY FATHER, WHEN MY TROUBLES SEEM IMPOSSIBLE, I WILL TRUST THAT YOU HAVE A "BUT GOD" ANSWER WAITING FOR ME. AMEN.

13

WHAT-IFS
AND WHAT IS

Give all your worries to him, because he cares about you.

1 PETER 5:7 NCV

YOU'RE NOT SICK, BUT there's this icky sort of feeling in your tummy. It doesn't happen every day. But some mornings, even the thought of getting out of bed and going to school has your tummy flip-flopping.

There's nothing particularly wrong. It's just, *what if* you wear the wrong clothes and other kids laugh? *What if* you say the wrong thing? *What if* the teacher calls on you and you have no idea what the answer is? Or *what if* all those things happen, your friends won't speak to you, and you're forced to sit alone in the lunchroom where everyone points and laughs at you?

What-ifs are usually the worst things we can imagine. They're hardly ever true, but they're one of the devil's favorite tricks. Because if you're worried and afraid, then you aren't being who God created you to be. The best way to get rid of *what-ifs* is to remember a few *what-is* truths: you're an amazing child of God, God loves you, and He's always ready to help.

Part of what makes *what-ifs* so scary is the way they zip around your brain. So get those runaway thoughts under control by writing them down. As you write, ask God to take care of each one for you. At the end of the day, check your list— and thank God for the ways He answered you. Remember: God's got this, and He's got you! *That* is what's true.

DID YOU KNOW?

Back in the late 1990s, a huge *what-if* threatened to turn the world upside down. It was called Y2K (which means "the year 2000"). You see, in the 1960s when computers became popular, computer programs left the "19" off the year's date. So, 1987 was simply "87." But as the year 2000 neared, people began to panic. *What if*, on January 1, 2000, all the computers that ran banks, power plants, and subways suddenly thought it was the year 1900 instead of 2000? Everything could crash! There was a lot of worrying, but in the end, nothing much happened. Like so many what-ifs, Y2K just went away.

DEAR GOD, PLEASE GET RID OF ALL THESE WHAT-IFS IN MY HEAD AND FILL MY THOUGHTS WITH WHAT IS TRUE INSTEAD. AMEN.

14

IDK IS OK

"Just as the heavens are higher than the earth,
so are my ways higher than your ways. And my
thoughts are higher than your thoughts."

ISAIAH 55:9 ICB

DK. **THAT'S TEXTING LANGUAGE** for *I don't know.* And I don't know about you, but there are a lot of things I don't know.

I don't know how many stars are in the sky. Or how deep the ocean is. Or how many things swim and splash through it.

I don't know, but God does. He knows how many stars are in the sky because He put them there. He even gave each one a name (Psalm 147:4). God knows every drop of water in the ocean and can measure exactly how deep it is with His own hand (Isaiah 40:12). He knows every dolphin, jellyfish, and tasselled wobbegong swimming in it.

There is *nothing* that God doesn't know. He knows how and when and why and where—and the answer to every question we could ever ask. Sometimes we can see and understand His answers, like how the earth spins in space to make our days and nights. But other times His answers are too big for us to understand, like how many stars are in space or even why sometimes bad things happen to good people.

When we don't understand or don't know the answers, it's okay to say, "I don't know." Because we know the God who has all the answers. And He's always working for good in our lives (Romans 8:28), even when we don't understand. One day we will know the answers, but until then, we can just trust Him.

DID YOU KNOW?

The tasselled wobbegong is a kind of shark that grows to about four feet long. The lacy "tassels" around its head help it blend in with the ocean floor. It's an *ambush hunter*, which means it hides and waits for its prey. When a tasty bit of prey swims by, the tasselled wobbegong opens its mouth and sucks it in. Yikes! These unusual sharks are most commonly found around the Great Barrier Reef near Australia.

DEAR GOD, I KNOW YOU HAVE ALL THE ANSWERS. I WILL TRUST YOU, EVEN WHEN I DON'T UNDERSTAND. AMEN.

SPEAK UP!

When you talk, you should always be kind and wise. Then you will be able to answer everyone in the way you should.

COLOSSIANS 4:6 ICB

GROWN-UPS. THEY CAN BE kind of hard to talk to sometimes. After all, they're older and taller. And they can do really cool things like drive cars, go to work, and eat as many cookies as they want without getting scolded by their mom.

There are times, though, when you need to talk to grown-ups, and not just your parents. Like ordering your own meal at a restaurant, talking to a teacher about a grade, telling a school counselor about a problem, or asking a neighbor if you can mow their yard or babysit.

What do you do when the thought of speaking up makes you feel kind of queasy inside? Try this: SPEAK UP!

- **S**—*Say* a little prayer, because that's always a good thing, right?
- **P**—*Plan* what you want to say and *practice* saying it.
- **E**—Look the person in the *eye*.
- **A**—Take a slow, deep breath of *air*.
- **K**—*Keep* your voice loud enough to be heard.
- **U**—*Use* your best manners. "Please" and "thank you" help a lot when you want a grown-up to listen to what you have to say.
- **P**—*Pause* to listen to what the grown-up has to say.

You may need a little courage to talk to grown-ups. (And always be sure your parents know who you're talking to!) But with a little practice, a lot of kindness, and some courage from God, you'll be chatting away in no time.

GET READY TO ROAR!

Parents are perfect for practicing talking to grown-ups. And it's easy to do. Think about all the things you talk about with your friends. Like what's happening in their lives, movies you've seen, or funny things that have happened. Guess what! Your parents like to talk about those things too. Have a chat with your parents every day. Be sure to listen as much as— or more than— you talk. And you'll find that your parents are interesting people too.

LORD, LET MY WORDS ALWAYS BE KIND AND HELPFUL—NO MATTER WHO I'M TALKING TO. AMEN.

16

WHAT GOD SEES

"God does not see the same way people see. People look at the outside of a person, but the LORD looks at the heart."

1 SAMUEL 16:7 NCV

WHEN YOU LOOK AT others, what do you see? The color of their eyes or hair? How tall they are or the clothes they wear? That's not what God sees.

One time God sent the prophet Samuel to Jesse's family to choose a new king for Israel. When Samuel first saw the oldest son, Eliab, he thought, "Yep! This is the guy!" Eliab was tall and strong, everything a king should be—or so Samuel thought. But God had other plans. He chose David, the youngest of Jesse's sons. Back then, the youngest kid never got picked for anything, except maybe for being picked on. But God wasn't looking at what people could see. He was looking at David's heart. God saw a boy who would always love Him, and He wanted all of Israel to follow David.

You may feel pressure to follow the super-cool kids. You know the ones. They've got the super-cool clothes and the super-cool phones. But what do the things they *do* and *say* tell you about their hearts? Maybe some of those kids are kind and honest. After all, super-cool kids can love God too. And love is what matters the most.

Having the courage to look past what others say is important. No, you can't see inside someone's heart like God can, but you can see what people say and do. And those things say a lot. Ask God to help you see the way He sees.

GET READY TO ROAR!

David loved the Lord so much that God called him "a man after my own heart" (Acts 13:22 NIV). It wasn't that David was perfect. He made *plenty* of mistakes! But David knew God could see his heart. So when he messed up, he asked God for forgiveness (check out Psalm 51 for an example). What about you? What does God see in your heart? Is anger or jealousy or selfishness sneaking around in there? If so, be like David. Tell God about those things you're thinking and feeling. Then ask Him to forgive you and fill your heart with His love and goodness instead.

LORD, TEACH ME TO SEE OTHERS THE WAY YOU SEE THEM. AMEN.

QUIET COURAGE

"She did what she could."

MARK 14:8 NIV

IF YOU LOOK ONLY at the heroes in movies, you might think being courageous means blasting onto the scene to save the day. Or saving the world from an alien invasion. Or taking out a dozen bad guys all by yourself. But real-life courage isn't always big and bold and in your face. Sometimes it's soft and small and quiet. Yet even quiet courage can be powerful.

Think about the boy who offered his food to Jesus. It took courage to give up his bread and fish when there wasn't any other food in sight, and his tummy was probably rumbling. But his quiet act of *sharing* helped Jesus feed thousands of people (John 6:1–14).

Then there was the woman at the dinner party who poured expensive perfume on Jesus' feet. Though it sounds a bit strange to us, to Jesus it was a beautiful and quietly courageous act of *worship*. Others scolded her, but Jesus praised her (Mark 14:3–9).

Another woman suffered from a terrible illness that caused her to bleed for many years. With quiet courage, she reached out to touch Jesus' cloak, *trusting* that He could heal her (Mark 5:25–34).

Sure, courage can be big and loud and change the world. But it can also be scooting over to make room for one more at your table, giving thanks for your lunch at school, or stopping to pray with a friend who is hurting. Whether it's sharing, worshiping, or trusting, courage is often as simple as quietly doing whatever you *can* do to love God and help others.

GET READY TO ROAR!

Quiet courage is all around you. You'll find it in the older widow who sings in the choir every Sunday, even though it's a struggle to travel to church. Or in the teacher who notices each student and helps them be their best. Or in the parents who give up what they want so you can have what you need. Who do you see showing quiet courage? Write a note to thank them.

HOLY FATHER, IN BIG THINGS AND IN ALL THE LITTLE EVERYDAY THINGS, PLEASE GIVE ME THE COURAGE TO DO WHATEVER I CAN TO HELP OTHERS. AMEN.

18 DARE TO DREAM

With God's power working in us, God can do much, much more than anything we can ask or imagine.

EPHESIANS 3:20 NCV

DO YOU KNOW THAT God has hopes and dreams for you? When He created you, He didn't just give you two arms, two legs, a nose, and a couple of eyeballs. He also filled you up with all kinds of wonderful gifts, talents, and abilities. Then He took all those gifts, talents, and abilities, and He wove them into a plan for your life. It's a good plan for you to do amazing things for Him and for His kingdom. In other words, God's got big dreams for you.

But are your dreams as big as God's dreams? Because it's easy to just wake up, go to school, and do the same things day after day. Have the courage to dream big with God—and then go after His dreams for you. There may be songs inside you waiting to be sung or stories waiting to be written. There could be horses to ride, people to encourage, inventions to create, or some other wonderful thing God created you to do—all so that you can show the world how amazing God is.

What do you love to read and talk about? What's your favorite subject in school? Start thinking about what interests you. Then dare to dream—because you can't even imagine all that God has created you to do!

DID YOU KNOW?

You've heard of Disney World, Disneyland and Walt Disney, right? Disney is huge! But it didn't start out that way. It all started because a man named Walt Disney dared to dream. When he first arrived in California, he only had $40 in his wallet and a dream. Then, one day, Walt sketched out a mouse named Mortimer—whose name was changed to Mickey—and he's been entertaining children of all ages ever since. What kinds of crazy-wonderful-amazing dreams has God put inside you? Go ahead. Dare to dream!

GOD, SHOW ME THE DREAMS YOU HAVE FOR ME—AND HELP ME TO FOLLOW YOU TOWARD THEM EACH DAY. AMEN.

19

PARDON THE INTERRUPTION

When we have the opportunity to help anyone, we should do it.

GALATIANS 6:10 ICB

INTERRUPTIONS HAPPEN *ALL* **THE** time. You're about to break your record on a video game when your mom asks you to take out the trash. You've been looking forward to hanging out with your friends on Saturday, then your grandparents come for a surprise visit. You've just settled down with your favorite snack and TV show when your brother wants to change the channel to a show you don't like.

We usually think interruptions are bad things. They keep us from doing what we want to do. But that's not how Jesus saw interruptions. And He was interrupted *a lot*.

There was one day that was especially full of interruptions for Jesus. First, a man named Jairus interrupted Jesus and begged Him to come and heal his sick daughter. On the way to Jairus's house, Jesus was interrupted by a woman touching his robe so that she would be healed. As Jesus talked to her, He was interrupted yet again by people telling Him that Jairus's daughter was already dead. That's three interruptions in just a few short verses!

I don't know about you, but I'd probably be a little upset by all those interruptions.

Not Jesus. He didn't get frustrated or say, "Sorry, I'm busy right now. Come back next Tuesday." No, Jesus went with Jairus, then stopped to help the woman, and then traveled to Jairus's house and raised his daughter back to life (Mark 5:21–43). You see, Jesus knew something we all need to remember: interruptions are often our chance to help others and serve God.

So take out the trash, visit with your grandparents, and hang out with your brother. Let interruptions be an opportunity to show love, not frustration.

GET READY TO ROAR!

Read the story of the Good Samaritan in Luke 10:25–37. Jesus used this story as an example of loving your neighbor, but it's also a good example of how to handle interruptions. The priest, the Levite, and the Samaritan each had their day interrupted by the man who was injured while traveling to the city of Jericho. Who handled the interruption in a way that pleased God? Why?

LORD, THE NEXT TIME MY PLANS ARE INTERRUPTED, SHOW ME HOW THAT INTERRUPTION COULD BE PART OF YOUR PLAN. AMEN.

20
STAND OUT!

Jesus Christ is the same yesterday and today and forever.

HEBREWS 13:8 NIV

JESUS NEVER CHANGES. NOT ever. He is always good, always loving, and always doing what God the Father says is right. You can count on Jesus because He is always Himself.

How about you?

Do you act like the same person at church and at home as you do at school? Do you use the same words with your friends that you use with your

grandma? Do you listen to the same music in your headphones as you do in your parent's car?

Or are you like a chameleon—an animal that changes color to blend in with its surroundings? Do you change who you are to blend in with the world around you?

Changing who we are to fit in can happen so easily, we might not even know we're doing it. Maybe we watch videos we know we shouldn't so that we don't feel left out when friends talk about them. Or maybe we're kind to that not-so-cool kid when she's at church, but we ignore her at school—or worse, laugh at her like everyone else.

God made you to stand out in this world by loving others and doing what He says is right. Sure, it takes courage to stand out, but don't forget you've got the Creator of the universe on your side to help you. Dare to be like Jesus. Be the same amazing child of God He made you to be—no matter where you go or who you're with.

DID YOU KNOW?

Blending in isn't the only reason chameleons change colors. They also change colors to show emotions like anger or fear. *Hmm*, that sounds kind of like us, doesn't it? Have you ever "changed your colors" when you're angry or afraid? Ask God to help you show how much you love Him, no matter how you're feeling.

DEAR GOD, I WANT TO STAND OUT FOR YOU. HELP ME BE BRAVE ENOUGH TO SHOW THE WORLD I AM YOURS—WHEREVER I GO AND WHOEVER I'M WITH. AMEN.

GAME OVER

"In this world you will have trouble. But be brave! I have defeated the world!"

JOHN 16:33 ICB

 OES IT EVER SEEM like the bad guys and girls are winning? The mean girl—the one who always turns up her nose at you—gets invited to the party you really wanted to go to. The bully who pushes you off the swings on the playground never gets caught.

When the bad guys and girls seem to be winning, remember this important truth: God's not finished yet. Yeah, there will be days when it seems like the devil and all the bad stuff he stirs up are bigger than the good stuff. The devil would love for you to think that the bad guys win and that there is no hope. But let me tell you a not-so-secret secret. It's one the devil really doesn't want you to know or believe. But it's the truth, straight from the Bible:

In the end, God wins.

And God doesn't just barely win. He doesn't cross the finish line just an inch or two before the devil does. The score isn't 99 to 98 with one second to go. God wins completely. No question about it; it's not even close. When Jesus rose from the dead, He beat the devil once and for all. Game over. And when you choose to be on God's team—to love and follow Him—you win too.

Yes, the devil is still fighting. Yes, he's still stirring up trouble for you. And yes, sometimes he seems to be winning. But you can be brave because you know the truth—in the end, God wins!

DID YOU KNOW?

One of the worst defeats in football history was way back in October of 1916. Georgia Tech defeated Cumberland College in Tennessee with a score of 222 to 0. Yes, you read that right. Cumberland didn't score a single point. They never even got close. It was a huge victory for Georgia Tech, but that's nothing compared to God's victory over the devil.

DEAR GOD, SOMETIMES IT SEEMS LIKE THE DEVIL IS WINNING, BUT I KNOW THAT'S A LIE. YOU'VE ALREADY BEAT HIM. AMEN.

22

A FRESH START

When I am afraid, I will trust you.

PSALM 56:3 ICB

STARTING OVER CAN BE tough. Especially when starting over wasn't your idea in the first place. Maybe your family moved, and now you've got to figure out a new neighborhood and make new friends. Or maybe you've graduated from one school and it's time to start a new one, with a whole new maze of kids and teachers to figure out. Or maybe you've started going to a new church, and there are all these different people and groups and expectations.

Whatever the reason, starting over can be hard. But it can also be exciting. Think of it as a fresh start. You have the chance to try new things and break out of your box. Instead of being the one who always eats peanut butter and jelly for lunch, you can be the one who sometimes brings sushi for lunch. Instead of just swinging on the monkey bars at recess, you can try playing soccer too. Instead of being the one who never speaks in class, you can be the one who isn't afraid to read or pray out loud.

When it's time to walk into that new lunchroom, classroom, or church, take a deep breath and say a little prayer. Ask God to help you be brave enough to be your best self. Remember that you're never alone, and take that first step—it's the hardest one. Then smile. Look people in the eye. Say hello. Introduce yourself. Be kind. Be helpful. Above all, be yourself— and soon you'll find that this starting over thing isn't so bad after all.

GET READY TO ROAR!

One of the biggest ways to make starting over easier is to remember people's names. But that can be tough, especially when you meet a lot of new people. Here's a trick to try: When someone tells you their name, repeat it back to them: *Hi, Ben, it's nice to meet you.* And when you leave, say their name again: *Bye, Ben!* Then the next time you see that person, you'll probably remember their name!

DEAR GOD, INSTEAD OF BEING AFRAID OF THE CHANGES AROUND ME, SHOW ME ALL THE CHANCES I HAVE TO DO SOMETHING NEW FOR YOU. AMEN.

23

WHEN THE WINDS BLOW

"Have courage! It is I! Do not be afraid."

MARK 6:50 ICB

IT WAS THE MIDDLE of the night, and the disciples were out in their boat on the lake. The wind was blowing so hard that, even though they rowed with all their might, they couldn't get to the other side. Suddenly, they saw a figure walking toward them on the water. They were terrified! Then a familiar voice called out to them and said, "Do not be afraid" (Mark 6:50 ICB). It was Jesus!

The instant Jesus stepped into the disciples' boat, the wind stopped roaring. Yeah, they were still in the boat out in the middle of the water, and they still needed to row to shore. But life suddenly got a whole lot calmer. Why? Because Jesus was with them.

And He's with you too. When you believe in and follow Jesus, He never leaves your side. And that's amazingly good news for you. Why? Because troubles and problems are going to blow through your life just like they did that night with the disciples.

Now, sometimes Jesus will instantly stop whatever storm or fix whatever problem that has crept into your life. He has the power to do that—just like when He instantly stopped the wind. Other times, He won't fix everything in an instant. Instead, He'll stay right there with you, helping you and guiding you safely through to the other side. He can calm the storm for His child, but He can also calm His child in the storm. And just like those disciples, your life will be a whole lot more peaceful.

DID YOU KNOW?

That stormy night, the disciples were out on the Sea of Galilee. But the Sea of Galilee isn't really a sea at all. It's actually a freshwater lake. It's surrounded by hills and mountains where the air is cool and dry. But close to its shores, the air is warm and moist. At times, the cool air and warm air can crash together, causing violent winds and storms— just like the ones the disciples found themselves stuck in that night.

LORD, THANK YOU FOR NEVER LEAVING MY SIDE, EVEN IN THE MIDDLE OF A STORM. AMEN.

24

GET AWAY WITH GOD

Jesus often slipped away to be alone so he could pray.

LUKE 5:16 NCV

JESUS CAME TO EARTH with the biggest, most important mission ever: to save us from sin and give us a way to heaven. So He was busy. *Really busy.* His to-do list probably looked something like this: teach the disciples, heal the sick, cast out a demon, raise Lazarus from the dead, and teach the disciples again.

Even though Jesus had a lot to do, He took time to be alone with God. Before He chose His twelve disciples, He spent all night in prayer (Luke 6:12). After teaching and feeding a large crowd of five thousand people, Jesus went off by

Himself to pray (Mark 6:46). And before He was arrested, He went to the garden of Gethsemane to pray (Matthew 26:36).

But it wasn't only during the big moments of His life that Jesus got away to pray. It was something Jesus did often. Now, if being alone with God was important to Jesus—who was perfect in every way—then it's safe to say it's pretty important for us too.

Yes, you can talk to God anytime and anywhere. He will hear you even in the middle of the noisiest crowd. But it's much easier for *you* to hear God when you find a quiet place to be alone with Him. It could be in your room, out on the swing set, or in the branches of your favorite tree.

Find a way to be alone with God every day. Talk to Him, pray, sing, and read His Word, and you'll discover just how special time alone with God can be. You can't have a quiet soul without quiet time.

GET READY TO ROAR!

Create your own "get away with God" space. It could be in the corner of your room, an empty closet, or wherever you can make a space. Be sure to put a Bible there. Add pens, paper, and colored pencils for journaling, drawing, and keeping a prayer list. Add a comfy pillow or chair. If you like to "get away" outside, keep your things in a tote bag and grab a picnic blanket to carry out with you.

HOLY FATHER, YOU ARE THE GOD WHO CREATED EVERYTHING— MOUNTAINS AND OCEANS, LIONS AND LAMBS. AND YET YOU WANT TO SPEND TIME WITH ME. THANK YOU. AMEN.

25

WHAT ARE YOU WAITING FOR?

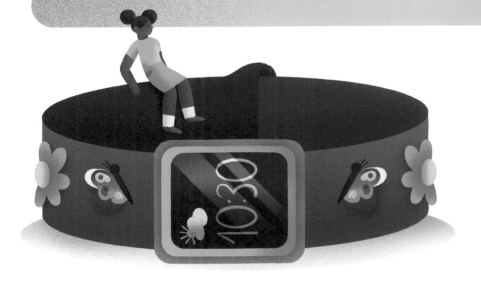

> When a person knows the right thing to do,
> but does not do it, then he is sinning.

JAMES 4:17 ICB

E WAIT OUR TURN in line, we wait for the end of class, and we wait at the doctor's office. There are times when we have to wait, and being able to wait patiently is a good skill to have.

But there are times when we *shouldn't* wait, when waiting isn't the best choice. Like when we wait to do what is right. The Bible says this kind of waiting is a sin (James 4:17).

Why would we ever wait to do what is good and right? Maybe it's because . . .

- We're afraid people will make fun of us, so we wait to make friends with that kid everyone else laughs at.
- We think we have a right to stay angry at our brother or sister for breaking our favorite toy, so we wait to forgive.
- We'd rather spend the afternoon playing video games or hanging out with friends, so we wait to clean our room, even though our parents asked us to.

One of the biggest reasons we wait to do what's right, though, is this: *We think that if we wait long enough, someone else will do it for us.* And maybe they will. But we'll have missed out on a wonderful opportunity to do what God says is best.

Is there a good and right thing that you're waiting to do? Well, what are you waiting for?

DID YOU KNOW?

We humans do a lot of waiting. The average person will spend anywhere between six months and two years of their life waiting in lines. These days there's even a line to get to the top of Mount Everest, the world's tallest mountain. Hikers might spend two hours or more waiting in a line to finish the last bit of their climb to the top!

LORD, FORGIVE ME FOR THE TIMES WHEN I WAIT TO DO WHAT IS GOOD. HELP ME HURRY TO OBEY YOU. AMEN.

26

DON'T FORGET YOUR WARM-UP!

First I prayed to the God of heaven.

NEHEMIAH 2:4 ICB

PORTS PLAYERS DO SOME pretty crazy things to warm up before they face their opponents. One famous football player dances to loosen up his muscles. Another athlete munches on exactly *two* chocolate chip cookies. Others will do anything to keep a winning streak going, including refusing to change their shirts or their socks. *Pee-ew!*

Maybe you aren't headed out onto the sports field, but you *are* headed out to face an opponent every day—the Evil One himself. And every day is a battle. What should you do to "warm up" for the fight? An Old Testament fellow named Nehemiah gives us the perfect answer.

Nehemiah was the cupbearer for the king of Persia. This was during the time when the Israelites were captives of the Persians. When some Israelites were allowed to return to their homes in Jerusalem, they sent back word that the city and its wall were in shambles. Nehemiah was heartbroken and wanted to ask the king to help Jerusalem. But first Nehemiah did a very important thing: he prayed. Nehemiah knew it would be a battle to rebuild Jerusalem, and he would need God on his side every step of the way.

Whether you're headed out to do something big or just headed off to school, you're going to need God on your side every step of the way too. So do what Nehemiah did to warm up—before you take a step, stop and pray.

GET READY TO ROAR!

Every day you're headed into battle. And every day the Evil One will try to trick, trip, or trap you. Create your own morning warm-up routine to get ready for the fight. Here are some ideas: As you stretch your arms up to the ceiling, stretch your prayers up to God. As you stretch out your legs and toes, read a verse—or a few—from the Bible. As you get dressed, ask God to cover you with His protection. And as you march off to breakfast, sing a song of praise to Him.

GOD, I'M STOPPING EVERYTHING I'M DOING RIGHT NOW TO SPEAK WITH YOU. HELP ME FACE EACH BATTLE SO I HONOR YOU ALL DAY. AMEN.

27

GOOFS, MISTAKES, AND MESS-UPS

The Lord's love never ends. His mercies never stop. They are new every morning.

LAMENTATIONS 3:22–23 ICB

YOU MIGHT AS WELL face it: you blew it. You flunked the test, you said the absolute wrong thing, you took the game-winning shot but missed. You started a fight with your brother or disobeyed your parents. You fell down in front of your classmates. Whatever it was, you completely goofed.

Do you know what, though? It happens to everyone. In fact, it happens all the time. So don't let your goof get you down. Don't let your mistake stop you from trying again. Because here's the thing you need to know about mess-ups: it's what you do next that matters most.

Think about Peter. When Jesus was arrested, Peter, one of Jesus' friends and disciples, didn't stand by His side. He was scared and stood back at a distance. And when people asked Peter if he was friends with Jesus, he said he didn't know Jesus—*three times*! Talk about failure. But watch what Peter did next. Okay, sure, first he cried over his mistake. It's okay to be upset for a little while. But a few days later, when Jesus rose from the grave, Peter was already back with the disciples (Luke 24:9–12). And when Jesus gave him a mission—to teach and take care of His people— Peter went out and did it (John 21:15–19).

When you mess up, face-plant, or just generally goof, it's okay to be upset—for a little while. Then it's time to remember that God is all about second chances. So get up, dust yourself off, and give it another try.

DID YOU KNOW?

Back in the early 1900s, people heated their homes by burning coal, which left dark, sooty dirt all over their wallpaper. The Kutol company made a putty that cleaned the wallpaper, and it worked great. But then in the 1950s, people switched to a much cleaner electric heat. They didn't need the putty anymore, and the company struggled. Then one day the owner's sister-in-law discovered that her preschoolers loved playing with the stuff. That's how Kutol putty got its second chance—as Play-Doh!

LORD, I'M SO THANKFUL FOR YOUR SECOND CHANCES. WHEN I MESS UP, HELP ME GET BACK UP AND TRY AGAIN. AMEN.

28

I'M SORRY

We all make many mistakes. If there were a person who never said anything wrong, he would be perfect.

JAMES 3:2 ICB

YOU SEARCHED EVERYWHERE FOR your favorite shirt. When you couldn't find it, you yelled at your sister, "You borrowed it and lost it!" Then . . . you found it at the bottom of your closet, near your old backpack. Now your sister is super-mad at you.

Or maybe you thought you were being funny when you made that joke about your friend, and everyone laughed. But now your friend feels hurt and embarrassed.

Or you were supposed to finish all your chores before bedtime. You even *promised* your parents you would do them, but you didn't. And now your dad is disappointed in you.

Whatever it was, you know you were wrong. And now you need to apologize. You need to admit you've messed up and try to make things right again. But you really don't want to. Why is it so hard to say, "I'm sorry"?

None of us likes to admit when we've goofed. And we might be worried about what the other person may say back to us. What if they're angry or upset? What if they say that "I'm sorry" just isn't good enough?

It takes courage to admit when you've messed up. And it takes courage to ask someone to forgive you. But it's what God asks us to do. The Bible even tells us that if we're about to do something for God and remember that someone is upset with us, we need to stop and go make peace first (Matthew 5:23–24).

Nobody is perfect. You're going to mess up, and you're going to need to apologize. The quicker, the better. Be humble. Be honest. Then do all you can to make the wrong right again.

GET READY TO ROAR!

The next time you need to say you're sorry, try writing it in a note. Explain that you know you were wrong, and you want to make it right. Ask the person to forgive you. Add a drawing or a pretty picture to go along with your note. Then deliver it with a hug, a smile, and an "I'm so sorry."

GOD, SOMETIMES I NEED TO SAY "I'M SORRY" TO YOU. PLEASE FORGIVE ME FOR THE WRONG THINGS I'VE DONE. AMEN.

29

THE COURAGE TO FORGIVE

**If someone does wrong to you, then forgive him.
Forgive each other because the Lord forgave you.**

COLOSSIANS 3:13 ICB

HEN YOU'VE BEEN HURT, it's okay to feel angry for a little while. You don't have to pretend that everything is all right. But be extra careful with your words and actions when you're hurting. You don't want to say or do something that makes things even worse.

Oh, and there's one more thing—you need to forgive the person who hurt you.

Forgiving someone doesn't mean what they did was okay. And it doesn't mean everything goes back to the way it was before, either. It might, or it might not. Your friendship may need to change. It may even need to end. (A parent or trusted adult can help you figure that out.) Forgiveness can happen right away, or it might take a little time and prayer. If it's a big hurt, it might take *a lot* of time and prayer. That's okay too.

Giving forgiveness to someone isn't always easy. In fact, it rarely is! And it usually takes some courage. Sometimes it's easier to just stay mad and hold a grudge. Especially if the person refuses to say they're sorry. Or if they say they did nothing wrong. What do you do then? Forgive them anyway. Because forgiving is more about emptying the anger out of your own heart than it is about them.

LORD, IT'S EASY TO STAY ANGRY. HELP ME DO THE HARD WORK OF FORGIVING INSTEAD. AMEN.

GET READY TO ROAR!

Want to know how fast God whisks away your sins when you ask Him to forgive you? Try this experiment: You'll need a small bowl, water, dish soap, and black pepper. Fill the bowl with water. Sprinkle on some black pepper. (Not too much—be sure you can still see the water.) Cover your finger with dish soap and then touch the water in the bowl. Did you see how fast the pepper flew away? When you tell God you're sorry, His forgiveness is even faster!

30

USE THE MIC!

He comforts us every time we have trouble, so that we can comfort others when they have trouble. We can comfort them with the same comfort that God gives us.

2 CORINTHIANS 1:4 ICB

HAVE YOU EVER SPOKEN into a microphone? It makes your voice so much louder! And troubles can do the same thing.

Most days you can do a pretty good job showing the world how awesome God is. But when you're in the middle of a trouble, your "voice" gets louder—like someone just handed you a mic. That's because when the world knows you're a Christian, they pay extra-close attention to how you handle the messy parts of life. They want to see if you really do trust Jesus. So . . .

- When you lose your starting spot on the team, do you sulk and throw a fit? Or do you cheer on those who are playing?
- When your family vacation is canceled because there's not enough money, do you fuss and complain? Or do you thank your parents for all the ways they take care of you?
- When someone you love is sick, do you talk about how unfair it is? Or do you praise God for the doctors, nurses, and medicines that can help?

Trust God with your mess, and let Him turn it into a message. No, you didn't ask for the microphone of your trouble, but now you've got it. So be brave enough to use it. The courage you show just might help someone else be courageous too.

DID YOU KNOW?

When Frank Sinatra—one of the most popular singers of all time—first started out, he sang through a Rudy Vallee megaphone. But people in the audience would sometimes try to throw pennies into it as he sang! To avoid choking on the pennies, Sinatra moved around a lot as he sang. At last, he was able to purchase his first microphone for $60, which allowed him to sing without worrying about flying pennies!

LORD, WHEN EVERYTHING SEEMS TO GO WRONG, HELP ME SHOW THE WORLD HOW MUCH I STILL LOVE AND TRUST YOU. AMEN.

31

WHO YOU REALLY ARE

I praise you because you made me in an amazing and wonderful way. What you have done is wonderful. I know this very well.

PSALM 139:14 ICB

DO YOU KNOW WHO you are? Sure, you know your name, your address, and your parent's cell phone number. You memorized all that stuff back in kindergarten. But do you know who you *really* are? Because the devil hopes you don't. In fact, he's hoping you never find out— and if you do, he hopes you don't believe it.

So, who are you? *You are a child of God.* No matter what you might hear, you didn't come from some lightning-zapped puddle of mud. And you didn't come from fish or apes. God formed you on purpose with His own hands.

It takes a little courage to believe that, though. Because the world is more than ready to tell you that you don't matter much, that you're just an average, ordinary kid. You might even feel pretty average and ordinary. Maybe you have the Cs on your report card to prove it. Or maybe you've been picked on and put down by others so much that you're starting to believe the things they say about you.

Don't. Just look at the cross and see how important you are to God. He sent His only Son to die for you. Not some heavenly messenger. Not an army of angels. He sent Jesus.

There is nothing normal or ordinary about you—and that's a good thing! You are a child of God. *That's* who you really are.

DID YOU KNOW?

Before mirrors, people looked into pools of water to see what they looked like. The first mirrors were made from polished obsidian (ub-SID-ee-un), a kind of dark glass formed by volcanoes. Later, mirrors were made from copper, gold, silver, or even lead. Our mirrors today are made by spraying aluminum or silver onto the back of a piece of glass. But the very best mirror is the Bible. Its words show you exactly who you are—and who God wants you to be.

LORD, WHEN SOMEONE TRIES TO TELL ME THAT I DON'T MATTER, REMIND ME WHO I REALLY AM: YOUR CHILD! AMEN.

32

LIKE A LAMB

**He tends his flock like a shepherd: He gathers the lambs
in his arms and carries them close to his heart.**

ISAIAH 40:11 NIV

WHEN A LAMB IS frightened, it runs away. And even though it would be safer for the lamb to run toward the shepherd, some-times it runs the wrong way and gets hurt. When a lamb is hurt, the shepherd doesn't leave it to just take care of itself. No! The shepherd will gently lift the lamb up and carry it back to the safety of the flock.

When troubles come our way, we can act a lot like a frightened lamb. Instead of running to God, our Shepherd, it's tempting to run the wrong way—to friendships that aren't good for you, or to spending too much time on the internet or watching TV. You might start to think God has left you to face your troubles all by yourself. He hasn't, and He never will (Deuteronomy 31:8). That's His promise to you. And God never, ever breaks His promises (Numbers 23:19).

Talk to God about whatever is troubling you. You can tell Him all the things you can't tell anyone else. Whether it's troubles at school, at home, or with friends, God understands. And as you tell Him all your troubles, He scoops you up like a little lamb and carries you close to His heart . . . until you're ready to stand again.

DEAR GOD, THANK YOU FOR LISTENING TO ALL MY TROUBLES. PLEASE HELP MY HEART FEEL BETTER. AMEN.

GET READY TO ROAR!

Isaiah 40:11 gives the most beautiful picture of God as your Shepherd. He scoops you up like a little lamb and carries you close to His heart. Close your eyes and imagine you are that lamb. Curl into the warmth of His presence. Now draw a picture of what you've imagined. Write the words of Isaiah 40:11 on your picture to help you remember how much God loves and cares for you. Keep it in a special place in your room so that you can remember God is carrying you.

33

BETTER TOGETHER

Two people are better than one. . . . If one person falls, the other can help him up.

ECCLESIASTES 4:9–10 ICB

A **GROUP OF LIONS IS** called a *pride*. A bunch of frogs is called an *army*. A cluster of elephants is called a *parade*, while giraffes gather in a *tower* and gorillas in a *band*. So what's a group of Christians gathered together called? A *church*.

Animals stick together in groups for lots of reasons. They share their food, protect and take care of each other, and simply enjoy being together. And those are exactly the same reasons God created the church. Christians should share what we have, protect and care for each other, and simply enjoy being together.

But as Christians, we have even more reasons to stick together. We can sing together, pray together, and praise together. We can laugh and serve and encourage each other. We can help each other up when we fall. And we can help each other be brave when things get tough or scary. The fact is, we're stronger together, which makes it tougher for the devil to trip us up. That's why church is so important and God doesn't want us to miss out on gathering together (Hebrews 10:25). Because He knows that life and faith are better when we're together.

LORD, THANK YOU FOR THE GIFT OF CHURCH AND FOR ALL MY FRIENDS AND FAMILY THERE. AMEN.

DID YOU KNOW?

Cheetahs are known for their speed. They can run up to seventy miles per hour, making them the fastest land animal on the planet. But one thing you may not know about cheetahs is that they are very shy. They struggle to make friends with other cheetahs. But zookeepers have found an unusual answer to this problem. When there is a new cheetah cub at the zoo, the zookeeper puts a dog with the cheetah cub to be its friend. Because the dog (often a Labrador retriever) is so friendly and outgoing, it teaches the cheetah to be more outgoing too. Now that's an extraordinary friendship!

34

PRETTY RADICAL

"I say to you, love your enemies. Pray for those who hurt you."

MATTHEW 5:44 NCV

THERE HE IS—THAT kid from PE class. You know the one. He likes to trip you on the playground so that everyone laughs. You decide to turn around and go the other way, but just then you see something. The bully stumbles and hits the ground with a *splat!* He tripped over his own feet! The other kids start to laugh, and honestly, you think about laughing too. But you don't. Instead, you walk over, stretch out your hand, and help him up.

Sure, it would've been easy to laugh like all the other kids, but that verse from Sunday school last week just popped right into your head: "Love your enemies. Pray for those who hurt you" (Matthew 5:44 NCV). And laughing when that kid face-planted in front of everybody would not be at all loving.

When someone hits you or laughs at you or trips you, Jesus asks you to do something pretty radical: love them anyway. Don't hit back, laugh back, or send them sprawling. In other words, don't pay back evil with more evil (1 Peter 3:9). Now, if someone hits you, that doesn't mean you can't take a step back out of striking range. Jesus doesn't expect you to be somebody's punching bag. Just don't punch back. Pray instead. Return their meanness with kindness—from a safe distance, of course. And trust Jesus to make everything right in His own time and in His own way.

GET READY TO ROAR!

Jesus didn't just tell us how we should live. He showed us. His enemies beat Him, told lies about Him, spat upon Him, and nailed Him to a cross to die. But what did He do? Read Luke 23:34 to find out. Do you have an enemy? Someone who makes you miserable? Write out a prayer for your enemy. Ask God to show you how you can return their meanness with kindness.

GOD, WHEN SOMEONE IS MEAN, IT'S SO EASY TO WANT TO BE MEAN BACK. PLEASE GIVE ME THE STRENGTH TO BE KIND INSTEAD. AMEN.

35

TURN OFF THE DARK

You are living with crooked and mean people all around you. Among them you shine like stars in the dark world.

PHILIPPIANS 2:15 ICB

LL YOU HAVE TO do is watch a few minutes of the news—or take a walk down your school's hallway—to know that everything is not the way God created it to be. Yes, there are plenty of people trying to do what is good and right. But there also seems to be a lot of people who care only about themselves and getting what they want. And then there are others who are just plain mean.

Paul said, "You are living with crooked and mean people all around you" (Philippians 2:15 ICB). It was true when Paul was alive, and it's still true now.

But that's where you come in. Yep, you. Because when you love Jesus, and when you have the courage to share that love with the world around you, Jesus shines through you like a star shining in the darkness. Like a light that turns off the dark.

Turns off the dark. That's kind of a weird thing to say, isn't it? Usually we think about turning on a light, not turning off darkness. But that's exactly what you do when you

- pray for someone who is sick, hurt, or struggling with a problem;
- stand up for someone who is being picked on; or
- forgive someone who has hurt or betrayed you.

When you share the love of Jesus with the world, you take power away from the darkness. So what are you waiting for? Get out there and turn off the dark.

LORD, HELP ME SHINE THE LIGHT OF YOUR LOVE. AMEN.

DID YOU KNOW?

The moon might be more than 238,000 miles away, but it can shine so brightly that it "turns off the dark" of the night. The moon isn't really shining, though. It's only reflecting the sun's light. In the same way, the love and kindness you offer to others is a reflection of the love and kindness that Jesus offers to you. Yet that reflection is powerful enough to chase away the darkness—or turn off the dark. So how can you turn off the dark today?

36

ALONE IN A CROWD

"You can be sure that I will be with you always."

MATTHEW 28:20 ICB

HAVE YOU EVER FELT alone in the middle of a crowd? It sounds kind of crazy, doesn't it? But it happens sometimes.

Maybe it was when you were little and lost sight of your mom in a crowded store. Sure, there were lots of people around, but not the one person who mattered most to you. Or maybe it was when you went to a party and discovered you didn't know a single person there. Or maybe it was when you walked into class on the first day of school and realized that not one of your friends was in the same class.

Feeling lonely isn't always about how many people there are around you. It's more about how connected you feel—or don't feel—to the people who are there.

The thing is, you're never really alone. Not in a crowd and not even when no one else is around. That's because God is always with you, everywhere you go. The key is to feel connected to Him. How? It can be as simple as saying a quick prayer asking God to show you He is there. *He will answer.* He might pop a favorite verse or song into your thoughts. He might send over a friend—an old one or a brand-new one. Or He might whisper in your heart and say, *Hello! I'm here, and you are not alone.*

DEAR GOD, THANK YOU FOR ALWAYS BEING WITH ME. NO MATTER WHERE I GO, I KNOW I AM NEVER ALONE. AMEN.

GET READY TO ROAR!

The easiest way to shake off loneliness is to reach out to others who might be feeling the same way. Look around. Who's sitting by themselves? Who's looking a bit lost? Or who's pretending to tie their shoes for the twelfth time? Head on over and introduce yourself. You just might make a new friend.

37

COURAGE TO FAIL

"Whoever can be trusted with a little can also be trusted with a lot, and whoever is dishonest with a little is dishonest with a lot."

LUKE 16:10 NCV

IT WOULD BE SO easy. Just one little peek at your friend's paper. One right answer would make all the difference between flunking this test and passing it. The teacher isn't even looking. What would it hurt? *You.* It would hurt you. And deep down inside, you probably know that. Because you know that cheating is wrong. Even if the teacher doesn't catch you, others might see. And they will never completely trust you again. They won't trust you when you promise to keep their secret. They won't trust you when you tell them about that awesome thing your brother did. They won't trust you to do your part in the group project. And they definitely won't trust you when you tell them how amazing Jesus is. So it's really important that you be a person of honor and honesty all the time.

Jesus said that if we could be trusted with little things, like the answers on a test, then we could be trusted with bigger things, like His truth. But the opposite is true too. If we're willing to cheat on little things, it's easy for others to believe that we would cheat on big things too.

So, yeah, it would be easy to cheat, to sneak one little peek. But that's the coward's way out. It takes courage to fail, to admit you're not perfect. So be brave. Be honest. Don't sneak a peek.

FATHER, HELP ME TO SAY NO TO TEMPTATION. GIVE ME THE COURAGE TO NEVER CHEAT. AMEN.

DID YOU KNOW?

One of the most famous cheats in the Bible is Jacob. He and his mother, Rebekah, plotted to cheat his brother, Esau, out of their father's blessing. Their father, Isaac, was blind, so Jacob put on his brother's clothes so he would smell like Esau. Next, Rebekah covered Jacob's arms and neck with goatskins so he would be hairy like Esau. Then, Jacob tricked his father into blessing him instead of Esau. Read Genesis 27:41–43 to find out how Jacob's cheating scheme worked out for him. Hint: it made his life much harder, not easier!

38

YOU'VE GOT A PURPOSE

Everything you say and everything you do should all be done for Jesus your Lord. And in all you do, give thanks to God the Father through Jesus.

COLOSSIANS 3:17 ICB

YOU WERE CREATED BY God for a purpose. A great big, God-size purpose. Some people say it's a "calling."

So what's your purpose? In some ways, it's the same for everyone: to tell the world about how awesome God is and that He loves each of us so much that He sent Jesus to save us. But the way you live out your purpose is going to be different from everyone else's because God made you to be amazing, special, and one of a kind. I know I'm getting all mushy on you, but I'm dead serious. There is nothing even remotely close to ordinary about you or the purpose God has for you.

We can get stuck in thinking that our purpose has to be something huge—like starting a church, digging wells in Africa, or smuggling Bibles into dangerous countries. Don't get me wrong—those things are great! But we can live out our purpose in the everyday moments of life. It takes courage to do ordinary things like school, homework, practice, and chores in a way that gives God glory. It takes courage to miss ball practice so that you don't miss church. It takes courage to be kind to the kid, the teacher, or the neighbor who isn't so kind to you. And it takes courage to get up every morning and search for ways—big and small—to tell the world about God. But that's exactly what God created you to do.

GET READY TO ROAR!

Think about all the ordinary things you do each day, like chores, homework, practice, and school. How can you use those ordinary moments to tell the world something about your extraordinary God? Perhaps it's singing praise songs while you clean your room, helping a friend with homework, cheering on your teammates at practice, or checking the mail for your older neighbor. What can you do today?

LORD, I BELIEVE YOU CREATED ME FOR A PURPOSE. HELP ME LIVE IN A WAY THAT GIVES YOU GLORY. AMEN.

39

THAT'S A PROMISE!

What he says he will do, he does. What he promises, he keeps.

NUMBERS 23:19 ICB

HAVE YOU HEARD THE saying "An elephant never forgets"? Landmarks, good feeding spots, watering holes, other elephants— they don't forget a thing! But God's memory is even better. He never, ever forgets a promise. Not for one second. And that means you can count on Him. If God said He will do it, then He will.

Think of all the different promises God gives you in the Bible. Here are just a few of them:

- He'll always love you (Psalm 100:5).
- He'll listen to your prayers and answer you (Psalm 91:15).
- He'll give you His strength and power (Isaiah 40:29).
- He'll give you everything you need (Matthew 6:31–33).

Sometimes people make promises and try very hard to keep them. Like when your parents promise to take the family hiking on Saturday, but storms roll in. Your parents want to keep their promise, but they can't. Other times, people make promises and then decide they don't want to keep them. Like a classmate who promises to invite you to their sleepover, then decides to invite someone else. Some people even make promises they never plan to keep.

That doesn't happen with God. Nothing will ever stop God from keeping His promises. He keeps every one He makes. And that's a promise!

DID YOU KNOW?

Elephants have an amazing ability to remember. When two circus elephants met again after being apart for twenty-three years, they trumpeted with joy and "hugged" with their trunks. An elephant in the wild can remember and recognize up to thirty different members of its herd. They also remember facts about the land—such as where food and water can be found. In times of drought, older elephants who have already lived through such a time remember what they did to survive and move their herds to better areas. But not even an elephant's memory is as perfect as God's!

LORD, THANK YOU FOR REMEMBERING AND KEEPING YOUR PROMISES TO ME. AMEN.

40

YOU WANT ME TO DO WHAT?!

God is the one who saves me; I will trust him and not be afraid.

ISAIAH 12:2 NCV

YOU WANT ME TO do what?!" Can't you almost hear some of the Bible's heroes saying those words when they realize what God wants them to do?

Like Moses. He was just a shepherd, wandering around with his sheep, when God showed up in a burning bush. God told Moses to do all kinds of things that didn't make sense. Like go back to Egypt and rescue his people—the same Egypt he ran away from because Pharaoh wanted to kill him.

But one of the most amazing things God asked Moses to do happened at

the Red Sea. The Egyptians had finally let God's people go. But then the Egyptians changed their minds and chased after them. The Israelites were stuck between the Egyptian army and the Red Sea. It did *not* look good. So God told Moses to hold his staff out over the sea. *What?* There's an army chasing them down and Moses is supposed to stick out his staff? Well, Moses did, the Red Sea split right down the middle, and the Israelites escaped to safety.

Holding out a staff didn't make sense, but it was the perfect answer. One day God will ask you to do something that may not make sense—whether it's forgiving something that seems unforgivable, giving more than you think you can give, or something even bigger. When He does, trust that it's the perfect answer.

LORD, SOMETIMES THE THINGS YOU WANT ME TO DO DON'T MAKE SENSE TO ME. BUT YOUR WAY IS PERFECT, SO I'LL TRY TO ALWAYS OBEY YOU. AMEN.

GET READY TO ROAR!

Anyway. It's a powerful word, especially when it comes to being brave. Because sometimes God will ask you to do things that scare you a little. Not because He enjoys seeing you shake and shiver, but because He knows that by facing your fears and trusting Him you'll be able to do all the great things He has planned for you. Do you have a chance to do something for God, but it scares you a little? Maybe it's helping in a nursery class at church or reaching out to the grumpy lady in the cafeteria. Take a deep breath, say a prayer, and do it *anyway*.

41

WAS THAT A SQUIRREL?

"Martha, Martha, . . . only one thing is important. Mary has chosen the better thing, and it will never be taken away from her."

LUKE 10:41–42 NCV

DO YOU GET DISTRACTED? That's when you know you should be doing something—something important—but something *not* so very important steals your attention.

It's like what happened to—*Wait! Was that a squirrel?*

Sorry, I'm back now. What was I saying? Oh, yes. Distractions. It's like what happened to Martha. You see, Jesus and His disciples had visited Martha's house. While Jesus was busy telling the disciples all kinds of wonderful things about

God, Martha's sister, Mary, was plopped down right in front of Him, soaking up every word. But Martha didn't hear what Jesus was saying. All she could think about was how to feed all those people. There was bread to bake, meat to roast, veggies to chop. Who was going to set the table? Martha spotted Mary sitting by Jesus, and she got mad—so mad that she said, "Lord, don't you care that my sister has left me alone to do all the work? Tell her to help me" (Luke 10:40 NCV).

Jesus gently reminded Martha of something we all need to remember: spending time with Him is the most important thing we can ever do. He knew Martha's attention had gotten pulled away by the dinner she wanted to make for Him. She'd been distracted. Don't misunderstand—that dinner was a good thing, but it wasn't the most *important* thing.

Are you making time for the most important thing—Jesus? Or are distractions keeping you away? Take a few minutes every day to stop everything else you're doing and give your attention to Him.

LORD, WHENEVER I GET DISTRACTED, PLEASE PULL ME BACK TO YOU. AMEN.

GET READY TO ROAR!

Distractions are those things that pull our attention away from what we're trying to focus on. What distracts you from your time with God? Make a checklist of ways to remove distractions. You might try finding a quiet spot away from your siblings, turning off devices, making a list of homework and chores, or getting a snack. Then go spend time with God!

42

YOU'RE SURROUNDED!

Don't be afraid. The army that fights for us
is larger than the one against us.

2 KINGS 6:16 ICB

THERE'S AN INVISIBLE WAR going on all around you. It's a
war between good and evil, and it's as real as any war you read about
in history class. You fight this war every day when you decide to do
what's right. But you *never* fight alone. And long ago one man got to see the
ones who were fighting for him.

That man was the servant of the prophet Elisha. You see, that servant woke up one morning to find that he and Elisha were surrounded by enemies. He was terrified, but Elisha wasn't worried. He simply said, "Don't be afraid. The army that fights for us is larger than the one against us" (2 Kings 6:16 ICB). Then Elisha asked God to open the man's eyes so he could see. God did, and the servant saw that the hills around them were filled with horses and chariots made of fire. It was an army of angels—the army of God!

What you need to learn from this story is that the angels didn't show up when the servant's eyes were opened. They were there the whole time! And they're with you the whole time too. They cheer you on and help you stand up for what's right. They make sure the enemy doesn't get too close or strike too hard.

Yes, you're in a war, but you never fight a battle alone. And I'll let you in on a little secret—God wins!

DID YOU KNOW?

In Bible times, soldiers carried shields to protect themselves from the enemy's arrows. They were often made of wood and covered with leather. The leather could be soaked in water to help put out flaming arrows. God gives you a shield too. It's called the shield of faith (Ephesians 6:16). You see, the Enemy is constantly shooting arrows of doubts and temptations at you. But when you have faith and trust God to take care of you, His shield protects you.

LORD, WHEN I FEEL SURROUNDED BY THE ENEMY, REMIND ME THAT YOUR ARMY IS BIGGER AND STRONGER AND ALL AROUND ME. AMEN.

43

COURAGE AND FAITH

Faith means being sure of the things we hope for. And faith means knowing that something is real even if we do not see it.

HEBREWS 11:1 ICB

ALL THROUGH THE BIBLE—and all through life—God asks His people to be brave and bold. He knows it takes courage to do what's right in this world. Think about Esther, who needed courage to go to the king and beg him to save her people. Or Moses, who faced down Pharaoh again and again. Or the disciples who risked being stoned, beaten, and thrown in jail to tell others about Jesus.

How did these Bible heroes have the courage to do what God wanted them to do? *Faith*. It wasn't faith in themselves or their own strength. It was faith in God.

So what is faith? It's trusting in God and His goodness. It's knowing that He's bigger and stronger than any problem. And it's believing that God is always there, ready to help you do what is right (Isaiah 41:10).

Faith and courage are like two sides of the same coin. They can't really be separated. Because it takes a little courage to put your faith—your trust—in God. After all, you can't see or touch Him. But when you bravely put your faith in God and when you trust Him to help you do what is good and right, He pours His power and courage into you. Which makes your faith stronger, which gives you more courage, which makes your faith stronger, which gives you . . . well, you get the picture—a big, bold,strong, courageous faith!

DID YOU KNOW?

People often flip a coin to help them make a decision, like who gets to go first. (If you have an Amazon Alexa, ask her to flip a coin. She'll tell you if it's heads or tails.) One of the most famous coin flips in history was made back in December of 1903. Two brothers flipped a coin to see who would be the first to try out their new invention. Those two brothers were Orville and Wilbur Wright. Wilbur won, and he was the first to try flying their new airplane.

DEAR GOD, PLEASE SHOW ME WHAT IS GOOD AND RIGHT—AND THEN HELP ME BE BRAVE ENOUGH TO DO THOSE THINGS. AMEN.

44

FAMILY VS. FRIENDS

"Honor your father and your mother."

EXODUS 20:12 ICB

SOMETIMES BEING A KID is like being caught between a rock and a hard place—or at least being caught between your parents and your friends. You don't want to disappoint your parents, but you want to fit in with your friends. You want to do the things your friends are doing, but you don't want to disobey your parents. It's like a battle of *Family vs. Friends*. Who will win?

Maybe your struggle is over a TV show that all the kids are watching and talking about. Your parents don't want you to watch it because it doesn't honor

God. But one day you're at a sleepover and your friends turn on *that* show. This is your chance to finally figure out what everyone's been talking about! Your parents will never know. What do you do?

You know the right answer. It won't be easy, but you have to stand up to your friends. Ask to watch another show or play a game. Or hang out with a book in another room until the show is over. If that doesn't work, you may need to call your parents to take you home.

Remember, your parents always want the best for you, even if you don't quite understand some of their rules. They're the ones who'll be there for you long after some of your friends grow up and move away.

And here's a tip: a true friend won't ask you to disobey your parents. A real friend will help you do what's right. If your friend is encouraging you to do wrong, then they're not acting like a friend. And it's time to find someone who is.

GET READY TO ROAR!

God tells us to honor our parents, but what does "honor" look like? Here are some examples: Pray for your parents. Think good thoughts about them. Obey your parents' rules—whether they'll know you obeyed or not. Say good things about them. Ask for their advice. Thank them. And if they make a mistake, remember they're still learning too, and they don't always know exactly what to do. What are some other ways you can honor your parents?

DEAR GOD, I WANT TO OBEY MY PARENTS, EVEN WHEN IT'S HARD. HELP ME TO ALWAYS CHOOSE WHAT'S RIGHT. AMEN.

45

SERIOUS SNOOZING

He who guards you never sleeps.

PSALM 121:3 ICB

WE SPEND ABOUT ONE-THIRD of our lives sleeping. Now, that's some serious snoozing! Scientists have found that getting enough rest is just as important to our health as eating and exercising. Yet we put off sleeping. In fact, people are the *only* mammals who put off going to sleep. Unlike those super-sleepy sloths, which spend fifteen to twenty hours a day dozing, we stay up late to do homework, watch TV, play games, or chat with friends.

But another reason we don't always get enough rest is because worry keeps us awake. We toss and turn over what might not happen. We stress about what might go wrong.

That's such a waste! Because here's an amazing thing about God: He never sleeps. *Never*. He doesn't catnap or catch a little shut-eye. He doesn't take a break, a vacation, or even a day off. God doesn't rest because He never gets tired. He's always on the job.

What's God doing with all that awake time? Working in your life for good. That's what God is always doing, whether you're awake, asleep, or stuck somewhere in between, like in that boring class right after lunch.

That means you don't have to worry about anything. God's got it covered. No, you may not know exactly how, and you may not see it happening. But God is always there, and He's working out all your troubles for good. So get some rest. Turn your worries and fears over to God. He's going to be awake anyway.

DID YOU KNOW?

Winston Churchill, the famous prime minister who led Britain during World War II, was a big believer in the power of naps. It was his habit to take a nap right after lunch—he even changed into pajamas before crawling into bed. His nap was often followed by a second bath for the day. Churchill believed that napping allowed him to get more work done in a single day. His naps were so important that he even kept a bed in the Houses of Parliament so that he could rest before a big speech!

LORD, YOU KNOW ALL THE THINGS THAT KEEP ME AWAKE AT NIGHT. I GIVE THEM TO YOU AND TRUST YOU TO WATCH OVER ME WHILE I SLEEP. AMEN.

46

WITH ALL YOUR HEART

"Love the Lord your God with all your heart and with all your soul and with all your mind and with all your strength."

YOUR HEART IS WORKING all the time—your *whole* heart. Your heart doesn't say, "Hey, left side, you've been working pretty hard. Take today off." And it also doesn't declare, "Right side, I know you don't like working early in the morning, so why don't you sleep in tomorrow?" No, your whole heart keeps on working all the time so you can run, jump, and . . . well, live!

So when the Bible tells you to love God "with all your heart," think about how your whole heart works *all the time*. That's how God wants you to love Him—all the time and with everything you've got. You don't take a break from loving God just because someone makes fun of you for it. Or because loving Him means you don't watch that movie all the "cool" kids are watching. Loving God with all your heart means loving Him when everything is going your way and when absolutely nothing is going your way.

That kind of love takes courage. Big courage. Because this world doesn't love God—and they won't love you for loving Him (John 15:18–19). I know that's tough news to hear, but you need to know this. You need to be ready.

And you also need to know that you *can* do this. You can love God with all your heart. Not because *you're* super-awesome and amazing—even though you are! You can have the courage to love God with all your heart because He loves you with all of His (1 John 4:19). *All the time.*

GET READY TO ROAR!

Loving God isn't just a heart thing—it's a mind, soul, and strength thing too. Love God with your mind by studying and memorizing His Word. Love God with your soul by singing and praising Him. And love God with your strength by using your hands to help others. Write down at least one way you can love God with all your heart, mind, soul, and strength this week—and then do those things!

LORD, I DO LOVE YOU. TEACH ME ALL THE DIFFERENT WAYS I CAN SHOW THE WORLD HOW MUCH I LOVE YOU. AMEN.

47

DARE TO LIVE

"I came to give life—life in all its fullness."

JOHN 10:10 NCV

DO YOU KNOW WHAT it means to "coast"? Imagine you're riding your bike and headed down a little hill. You don't have to do a thing to keep moving, right? No pedaling. No work. You're coasting! It's super-fun—and super-easy.

But bikes aren't the only way we coast. Sometimes we coast through life. That is, we take the easy way out, don't challenge ourselves, and avoid things that make us work. For example:

- You know you can get a solid C on the test without even trying. You think, *Getting a C is okay,* so you don't bother to study.

- Your mom asked you to clean your room, so you shove stuff in the closet and sort of straighten your bed. That's good enough, right?
- You've got a fabulous idea for your art project, but it'll take a lot of time and work. So instead, you slap something together and call it done. Art is art, right?

Perhaps the worst place we coast through life, though, is when it comes to serving God. Maybe you think you're a pretty good person already. So why should you rake an older person's leaves on a Saturday? Or give part of your allowance to send Bibles overseas? Or give up video game time to spend time with God?

Why? Because Jesus didn't take the easy way out when He chose the cross. He chose the hard way out so that you could live your best life—not just coast through it. So do the hard stuff. Put in the work. Live a life that dares to love Him and serve others. Don't wait—do it today!

LORD, I DON'T WANT TO COAST THROUGH LIFE. TEACH ME TO LIVE WITH EVERYTHING I'VE GOT. AMEN.

DID YOU KNOW?

Who invented the bicycle? No one really knows! One of the earliest known "bicycles" dates back to 1418 and had four wheels. A later bicycle had no pedals and had to be pushed along. The *velocipede* (vuh-LAH-suh-peed) was popular in the 1860s. People called it the "bone shaker," and its steel wheels made for a bumpy ride! Then, in the 1870s, an Englishman named John Kemp Starley introduced the more modern bicycle. As bicycling became popular, so did racing. Madison Square Garden was once home to some of the biggest indoor bike races in the country.

48

A FISHING MISSION

Jesus called out to them, "Come, follow me, and
I will show you how to fish for people!"

MATTHEW 4:19 NLT

FISHING IN BIBLE TIMES wasn't just something to do on the weekend or a day off from school. Fishermen—like Peter, Andrew, James, and John—worked long, hard hours. It was their job, and they *needed* to catch lots of fish so they could sell them. That was how they took care of their families. So when Jesus called out, "Come, follow Me," that wasn't an easy thing for those first disciples to do.

Dropping everything to follow Jesus took some courage. Those guys left their jobs, their families, their homes—everything they knew—and followed Jesus, a guy they had just met. If He had been anyone other than the Son of God, we would say they were crazy. Some people would still say they were crazy. And they might say the same thing about you when you set out to follow Jesus.

Don't let that stop you.

Because Jesus had a mission for those first disciples, and He's got the same mission for you. Instead of fishing for, well, *fish*, Jesus wants you to fish for people. No, you're not going to need any fishing nets for this kind of fishing. Instead, Jesus wants you to "fish" by sharing with others the message of who He is and why He came—because some people will be "caught" by God's love. This is the most important mission ever! It's about saving souls. It's about making a difference in someone's life *forever*. And if someone says following Jesus is crazy, just smile and remember that you're on a fishing mission!

DID YOU KNOW?

What's the heaviest fish ever caught? It was a great white shark, caught back in 1959 off the coast of Australia. It weighed 2,664 pounds—or about as much as two cows! Amazingly, it took only about an hour to bring it in. One of the biggest freshwater fish ever caught was a huge freshwater stingray that weighed between seven hundred and eight hundred pounds. That nearly fourteen-foot monster was caught in Thailand in 2015.

LORD, NO MATTER WHAT I HAVE TO LEAVE BEHIND, I WANT TO FOLLOW YOU. AMEN.

49

SNEAK ATTACK

If any of you needs wisdom, you should ask God for it.

JAMES 1:5 ICB

LEOPARDS ARE CALLED *AMBUSH* predators. That means they sneak up on their prey and then *pounce*! Their spots help them hide in the shadows of the tall grasses and trees as they watch and wait for just the right moment. Their prey—baboons, monkeys, antelope, even snakes—don't even see them coming.

The devil is sneaky like that too. One of his favorite ways to sneak up on us is to hide the truth about sin. He tries to make wrong choices look right and right choices look wrong. He especially likes to take bad things and disguise them as something good or harmless, or at least not so bad. For example, he wants you to think you're not gossiping if you just tell *one* person your friend's secret. Or that you're not cheating by letting a friend copy your homework; you're just being helpful. Or that you're not lying; you're just trying to stay out of trouble.

When you see it written out like that, it's easy to spot the sin, isn't it? It's not so easy in life, though. So how do you spot those sneaky sins? Ask God to show you. He probably won't drop a flashing neon arrow that says, "Sin alert! Sin alert!" He's more likely to give your heart a gentle nudge that says, "Something's not right." When He does, pay attention, and ask God to give you the wisdom to get that sin out of your life.

LORD, OPEN MY EYES TO SEE ALL THE WAYS SIN TRIES TO SNEAK IN, AND THEN HELP ME TOSS IT BACK OUT AGAIN. AMEN.

DID YOU KNOW?

One of the most famous sneak attacks in history happened during the Trojan War between the ancient Greeks and the Trojans. After years of fighting, the Greeks pretended to accept defeat. They built a huge wooden horse and offered it as a victory trophy. The Trojans pulled the horse inside the city gates. When night fell, Greek soldiers climbed out of the horse, opened the city gates, and led the Greek army to victory. Scholars aren't sure exactly how much of that story is true. Why? Because it happened over a thousand years before Jesus was born!

50

TRUSTED WITH TROUBLE

You meant to hurt me. But God turned your evil into good. It was to save the lives of many people. And it is being done.

GENESIS 50:20 ICB

WHEN YOU'VE GOT TROUBLE in your life, it's easy to wonder, "Why me?" But what if God has *trusted* you with this trouble? Don't misunderstand—it's the devil who's to blame for everything evil and bad. But what if God has put you where you are and allowed this trouble into your life so that He could do something amazing *through you*?

That's exactly what happened to Joseph. First, his big brothers sold him to Egypt as a slave. Then, he was thrown into prison and forgotten *for years*.

Yet Joseph trusted God through all his troubles and kept trying to do the right thing. Because of that, God used Joseph's troubles to save thousands—maybe millions—of lives.

Now, chances are you're not headed off to prison in a foreign country like Joseph. But since everyone has troubles, sooner or later you'll have some too. That means you'll also have a chance to let God use those troubles to do something amazing. For example, if a friend hurts your feelings, you can help them learn how God forgives by choosing to forgive them. Or if you're having a day when everything goes wrong, you can show how much you love God by praising Him anyway.

So the next time troubles come your way, ask yourself this: *Is God trusting me with these troubles? Is this part of His bigger mission for me?* Then love, trust, and follow Him, and look for the good He brings out of your troubles. It's there—because that's a promise God has given to you (Romans 8:28).

GET READY TO ROAR!

Grab a favorite dessert recipe and gather up the ingredients. You've probably got things like eggs, flour, sugar, baking soda, and butter. By themselves, none of those ingredients are all that tasty. Who wants to eat a raw egg? Blech! With a grown-up's help, follow the recipe's instructions. Now all those ingredients taste wonderful! Life is kind of like that. Some of the "ingredients" aren't all that great by themselves. But when God puts them all together, they turn out amazing!

LORD, WHEN TROUBLES COME MY WAY, I'LL TRUST YOU TO BRING SOMETHING GOOD OUT OF THEM. AMEN.

51 PRICKLY PEOPLE

Love is patient, love is kind.

1 CORINTHIANS 13:4 NIV

HAVE YOU EVER HEARD the old joke about how you hug a porcupine? The answer? *Very carefully!* Okay, yeah, it's a pretty lame joke. But it's a little funny. It's also a little true—and not just with actual porcupines. You see, some people are kind of like porcupines—very prickly. Or grouchy. Or grumpy. Or whatever you want to call them. But the fact is that some people are harder to love than others.

Do you know what I've found? Those prickly people are often the ones who need love and kindness the most. So why do they make it harder to love them? My guess is that at some point, someone hurt them. And they don't ever want to be hurt like that again. So, like an angry porcupine, they bristle their quills and threaten to poke anybody who gets too close.

How do you love a prickly person? *Very carefully!* Or, as 1 Corinthians 13:4 puts it, with patience and kindness.

Now maybe you're thinking, *A lot of people are easy to love, so why do I need to love someone who's prickly?* That's an easy answer: because God is patient and kind to *you*. And let's face it: we all have our prickly days. So, yeah, it can take some courage, but be patient with those prickly people and offer them kindness every chance you get.

LORD, HELP ME SHOW PATIENCE AND KINDNESS TO EVERYONE, EVEN TO THE PRICKLY PEOPLE. AMEN.

DID YOU KNOW?

Porcupines are best known for their prickly quills. One porcupine can have up to thirty thousand quills! Those hard, sharp quills are made of *keratin* (KER-uh-tin), which is the same stuff your hair and nails are made of. Porcupines can't actually shoot those quills at their enemies. That's just a myth. But if a porcupine is attacked, the quills become loose and burrow deep into their attacker's skin. Ouch! Porcupines cause big problems for lions, though. When lions attack porcupines, they can end up with quills stuck in their nose or mouth. That makes it harder for them to sniff out and eat prey!

52

RUN TOWARD THE ROAR

"I am the LORD your God, who holds your right hand,
and I tell you, 'Don't be afraid. I will help you.'"

ISAIAH 41:13 NCV

WHEN YOU HEAR THE word *lion*, you might think of a big, fuzzy mane or super-sharp claws. Then, of course, there's that whole "king of the jungle" thing. But chances are, the first thing you'll think of is its roar.

A lion's roar is big and loud and *really scary*. Especially if you happen to be a cute little gazelle trotting across the African plains. Just hearing that sound will send a gazelle running as far away from the roar as possible. Which is the worst thing it could do!

Why? Because that roaring lion isn't where the most danger is. The real hunters are the lionesses, hiding in the tall grass behind the gazelle. You see, the lion's job is to creep out in front of the gazelle and *ROOAARR!*—making it turn around and run right into the middle of all those lionesses. *Gulp!*

As crazy as it sounds, the safest thing for the gazelle is to run *toward* the roar.

That's true for you too. When you run from the things that scare you—like trying something new, standing up for what's right, or telling someone about God—you actually move closer to the danger. That's because you're moving closer to what the devil wants you to do and farther away from what God wants you to do. Facing your fears is the best thing to do.

And guess what! You're not some cute little gazelle surrounded by lions and lionesses. You're a child of God, and you're always surrounded by Him. He'll help you face your fears. Trust Him. Be brave. And run toward the roar!

GET READY TO ROAR!

Is something roaring in your life right now? Something you're afraid to do? Maybe it's trying out for the team, singing a solo, or inviting a friend to church. Or maybe it's standing up to that older kid and telling him to leave the little kids on the bus alone. What's the first step you could take to run toward the roar? Talk to God about it, and then *run*.

DEAR GOD, WHEN FEAR IS ROARING AT ME, PLEASE GIVE ME THE COURAGE TO RUN TOWARD THE ROAR. AMEN.

53

PICK UP YOUR SWORD!

Take the sword of the Spirit, which is the word of God.

EPHESIANS 6:17 NCV

YOU'RE IN A BATTLE every day. It's a battle between good and evil, truth and lies. But don't worry! God wants you to be ready for the battle, so He's given you a sword. What? You don't see it? That's because it's no ordinary sword made of metal—it's much more powerful than that. It's the sword of the Spirit, also known as the Bible. *How can the Bible be a weapon?* Because it's filled—beginning to end—with God's truth. Those truths cut like a sword through the devil's lies. But you can't just grab a sword and charge into battle. You need to practice.

Think about it. That Olympic gymnast didn't walk out onto the mat one day, start flipping through the air, and win a gold medal. She probably started with a cartwheel—and it probably wasn't very good at first. And that professional basketball player didn't just show up at the game and swish a three-pointer. He spent years practicing his shots. Even Spider-Man had to practice swinging through the air.

But we know this, right? To be really good at tumbling, shooting hoops, web-slinging, or just about anything, we have to train and practice. Why would using the sword of the Spirit be any different?

You need to pick up your sword every day and train. How? Read it. Memorize its words. Practice using its truth—like when the world tells you money and fame are all that matters, pull out the sword of Matthew 6:24 and cut through that lie with the truth that putting God first is most important. It really is a battle out there—so get ready to use your sword!

GET READY TO ROAR!

In the US, Olympic gymnasts will train for roughly six hours a day, six days a week—for years! One professional basketball player takes at least three hundred shots every practice. Your faith is far more important than any sport or game. So how much are you practicing? Write out your own training schedule for how often you'll read the Bible and memorize verses—and stick to it!

LORD, THANK YOU FOR THE SWORD OF THE SPIRIT—THE BIBLE. TEACH ME TO USE IT WELL. AMEN.

54

YOU'VE GOTTA TRY THIS!

"I am doing a new thing!"

ISAIAH 43:19 NIV

YOU'VE GOTTA TRY THIS!" What's the first thing you think of when you hear those words? Do you want to dive right in and give it a try? Or do you worry about what might go wrong?

Sure, it's wise to think things through. And it can be wise to say no to something that might be dangerous, not good, or just not right for you. But it's *not* good to always say no to things just because you haven't tried them before.

God filled this world with good things for you to discover, explore, and experience. Whether it's going camping for the first time, giving the science team a shot, or trying your dad's new broccoli dish, be brave and bold and try something new. Don't let fear keep you from giving the adventures of this life a try. Go camping with your friend. Grab a beaker and a lab coat, and join the science team. Take a bite of that broccoli. When you try new things, there will be some that you love, some that you hate, and some that you decide just aren't for you. And that's all okay.

The next time you have a chance to try a new adventure, a new project, a new after-school activity, a new way to serve, or even a new food, don't let fear hold you back. The important thing is to just be willing to try. Because you just might find yourself telling all your friends, "Hey! You've gotta try this!"

GET READY TO ROAR!

Make a list of things you've always wanted to try. Maybe it's simple things like joining the chess club, eating Thai food, or cooking your own meal. Maybe it's daring things like jumping off the high dive or rock climbing. Or maybe it's spiritual things like leading a prayer or putting on a puppet show to teach younger kids about Jesus. Be brave and try something new this week!

GOD, WHEN THE CHANCE TO DO SOMETHING NEW COMES ALONG, GIVE ME THE COURAGE TO GIVE IT A TRY. AMEN.

55

KNOCKED DOWN

I do believe! Help me to believe more!

MARK 9:24 ICB

WE ALL GET KNOCKED down. Sometimes we land in the dust from a shove on the playground or a stumble during a game. Or maybe it was clumsiness with a bit of gravity thrown in.

Sometimes, though, our hearts and spirits get knocked down. A friend turns out to be not such a good friend. School isn't going well. There's a sickness or a loss. Whatever the reason, we feel like we're flat on the ground, trying to spit the taste of dirt out of our mouths. Staring up at the world after you've been knocked down can leave you with some questions. And you know what? That's okay—just take those questions to God (1 Peter 5:7).

Mark 9 tells the story of a dad whose son was being hurt by an evil spirit. While the boy was physically knocked down, the dad's heart was knocked down by watching his son suffer. The father asked Jesus if He could do anything to help, and Jesus replied, "Everything is possible for one who believes" (Mark 9:23 NIV). The father wanted to believe Jesus could heal his son, so he prayed, "I do believe! Help me to believe more!" (v. 24 ICB).

When life knocks you down, you don't have to have all the answers. In fact, you probably *won't* have all the answers. But there is One who does—Jesus! Believe in Him. And when that's hard to do, ask Him to help you believe even more.

LORD, GETTING KNOCKED DOWN MAKES IT HARDER TO BELIEVE. BUT I DO BELIEVE. HELP ME BELIEVE EVEN MORE. AMEN.

DID YOU KNOW?

When something falls—or gets knocked down—it's gravity that makes it keep falling. Gravity is also the thing that keeps us all from floating off into space. It's gravity that keeps the earth circling around the sun, and it's gravity that keeps the moon circling around the earth. Scientists know a lot about what gravity does, but they don't understand all of it. Colossians 1:17 does a pretty good job of explaining how it works, though. Look up it, and see who is really holding all things— even gravity—together. Here's a hint: it's God!

56

HELLO, NEIGHBOR!

"You must love your neighbor as you love yourself."

LUKE 10:27 ICB

HAVE YOU HEARD OF the greatest commandment? It's the big one—the one thing you *must* do if you want to be a follower of God. What is it? Love God (Luke 10:27). Pretty simple, right? But that greatest commandment isn't the *only* commandment. There's also the second greatest commandment: "Love your neighbor as you love yourself" (Luke 10:27 ICB).

In the verses that come after that command, Jesus uses a story to explain who your neighbor is. Turns out, it's not just the people living next door to

you. And it's not just the people you see around your neighborhood or at school. It's *everybody*.

It takes some courage to love God in a world that doesn't think that's a cool thing to do, and so does loving your neighbor. Because let's be honest: not all neighbors are easy to love. So how do you do it? How do you find the courage to love people who are different from you? Who are grouchy, rude, or just plain mean?

Here's the answer: you can be brave enough to love others—the different, the grouchy, the mean—because God loves you *and* because God loves them too.

So when you see that new kid who talks a little strange, or that neighbor who yells every time a ball lands in his yard, or that girl who spreads gossip about you, remember that you're looking at someone God loves. And let His love—for you and for them—give you the courage to be kind, to be helpful, and to be a good neighbor.

HOLY FATHER, HELP ME SEE EACH PERSON I MEET TODAY AS SOMEONE YOU LOVE. AMEN.

GET READY TO ROAR!

Take a walk around your neighborhood (with your parents or with their permission, of course!). As you walk by each home, say a prayer for each person living there. Ask God to help you show your neighbors that you love them and that God loves them too! Maybe it's helping an older neighbor plant flowers or carry in groceries. It might be playing with young children to give their parents a break. Or it could be simply smiling, waving, and saying, "Hello, neighbor!"

57

I CAN DO IT MYSELF!

Trust the Lord with all your heart. Don't depend on your own understanding.

PROVERBS 3:5 ICB

I CAN DO IT MYSELF!" Do you ever say that? Whether it's roller-blading to a friend's house or doing your homework without your parent's help, we all like to prove how independent we are.

Growing up is all about becoming more and more *independent*, but growing up in your faith is all about becoming more and more *dependent* on God.

Sure, there are lots of things you can do by yourself, and you're learning more stuff all the time. Yet—and this sounds crazy—the more you learn to do on your own, the more you'll see how much you *can't* do on your own. Things like loving your enemies, being patient with your brother or sister, and having joy on hard days. Because no matter how grown-up you are, those kinds of things are impossible to do *on your own*. Yet they're completely possible with God. And there's one more super-important thing you can't do on your own: forgive your own sins. Don't worry, though. God's got that covered too. That's why He sent Jesus to die on the cross—to save you.

So keep learning and figuring out how to do new things. But don't ever be so independent that you forget to depend on God.

DEAR GOD, DON'T EVER LET ME GET INDEPENDENT THAT I FORGET HOW MUCH I NEED YOU! AMEN.

DID YOU KNOW?

On July 4, 1776, the Declaration of Independence declared that America would no longer be ruled by Great Britain—or did it? Actually, it was on July 2, 1776, that the Continental Congress voted for independence. July 4 was the day that the Congress officially adopted the words of the Declaration of Independence, but even that wasn't the day everyone signed it. Some didn't sign it until August 2 or even later!

58

JUST A LITTLE SIN

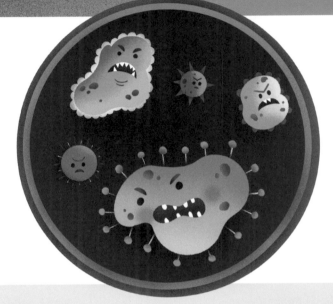

Jesus, God's Son, cleanses us from every sin.

1 JOHN 1:7 NCV

THESE DAYS, WE KNOW all about germs, but there was a time when people didn't know germs even existed! Doctors didn't worry about washing their hands, not even before surgery. When wounds became infected—which they often did—it was blamed on invisible, poisonous gases floating in the air.

Then, in the 1860s, along came an English surgeon named Joseph Lister. He believed tiny organisms called *germs* were getting into wounds and causing the infections. Lister experimented with chemicals to kill the germs and invented the first antiseptic. He also told doctors to wash their hands and wear gloves. The result? Fewer infections! (The name Lister may sound familiar; it's because Listerine mouthwash was named after him!)

Germs aren't the only tiny things that cause trouble—so can "tiny" sins. It's easy to tell yourself that a little fib isn't *really* a lie. Or listening to that song is okay because it only has a couple of bad words. Or that it's no big deal that you didn't clean your room like your mom asked because you'll do it later.

The truth is, there's no such thing as a little sin. There's just *sin*. And if you let a little bit in, it can grow bigger and more dangerous, just like a deadly infection. That's why God sent Jesus to wash away our sins. Do your best to stay away from sin. But if you mess up, confess your sin to Jesus and let Him make you clean again.

LORD, I KNOW THERE'S NO SUCH THING AS A BIG SIN OR A LITTLE SIN. PLEASE FORGIVE ME FOR THEM ALL. AMEN.

DID YOU KNOW?

There are four different kinds of germs: bacteria, viruses, fungi, and protozoa. *Bacteria* are tiny single-celled creatures that live *everywhere*. Some are good and helpful, but others cause diseases. *Viruses* are so tiny, they aren't even a whole cell. They need to invade other cells to live. *Fungi* are made up of multiple cells and are kind of like plants, except they can't make their own food. They need to grow on something, like trees or dead plants. *Protozoa* live in water and eat bacteria. But the best way to get rid of any germ is to wash your hands!

59

THE SUNSHINE TIMES

**I will give thanks to you, LORD, with all my heart;
I will tell of all your wonderful deeds.**

PSALM 9:1 NIV

IF YOU'VE EVER GOTTEN caught outside in the middle of a storm, you know it's a scary place to be. The wind howls, rain hammers down, lightning flashes, and thunder booms. When you're scared or when you need God's help, it's pretty easy to remember to pray! And while that's *definitely* a great time to talk to God, it shouldn't be the only time we turn to Him.

We need to turn to God in the good times too—when everything is going our way, when the skies are blue, and when there isn't a cloud in sight.

The danger of the sunshine times is that we start to think we've got this whole "life" thing under control. We've got it all figured out, and we can handle whatever comes our way. It's easy to just go skipping along and forget about God because we don't think we need Him right now. But the fact is, we need God just as much in the sunshine times of life as we do in the storms. Because He's the one who's really in control.

So when your day is full of sunshine and blessings, turn to God. Thank Him for all the goodness in your life. Keep spending time with Him. And know that He is with you in the sunshine as well as in the storms.

LORD, THANK YOU FOR BEING WITH ME EVERY DAY, EVEN WHEN EVERYTHING IS GOING RIGHT. AMEN.

GET READY TO ROAR!

When everything is going your way and life is one blessing after another, enjoy those times. Soak them up and *remember* them. Start a list, a journal, or a scrapbook to keep a record of all the good gifts God pours into your life. Then, when the clouds roll in and the storms of troubles strike, look back through your book of blessings. And remember that God is always good and faithful, and He will bless you again.

60

SUPERNATURAL

**Why am I so sad? Why am I so upset? I should put my hope
in God and keep praising him, my Savior and my God.**

PSALM 42:11 NCV

SO YOU DIDN'T MAKE the team you spent weeks practicing for. You
flunked the test even though you studied hard. Your mom got called in
to work, and that trip you've been dreaming of is suddenly canceled.
Life comes with so many good things, but it also comes with disappointments.

When things don't go the way you had planned, what do you do? Do you
mope around all sad and gloomy? Do you complain or throw a fit? After all,
you're upset—it's only natural to show it, right?

What if you chose to do something *super*natural instead? Now, when I say supernatural, I'm not talking about ghosts or magic or nonsense like that. I'm talking about doing something bigger and better than what people usually do. Like praising God or looking for something good in the middle of your disappointment or showing others how good God is through the way you act.

Okay, you didn't make the team. So cheer on your friends who did. Yeah, you flunked the test, but a number on a piece of paper doesn't make you any less wonderful to God. And missing the trip was a bummer, so why not think of something closer to home that your family can do together?

When you're disappointed, don't do what seems natural. Do the *super*natural thing.

DEAR GOD, WHEN THINGS DON'T GO THE WAY I WANT THEM TO, HELP ME REMEMBER ALL THE REASONS I HAVE TO PRAISE YOU. AMEN.

DID YOU KNOW?

What does Abraham Lincoln's beard have to do with board games? It all started with a man named Milton Bradley. He was a talented lithographer (a kind of printer), and one of his bestselling prints was a portrait of Abraham Lincoln. A *beardless* Abraham Lincoln. When Lincoln grew a beard, no one wanted the beardless prints anymore. It was a pretty disappointing time in Bradley's life. In fact, he had to find another way to make a living. He created a board game called The Checkered Game of Life, which later became simply The Game of Life. Thankfully, it was a hit! His company went on to create several other games you might have played, including Candy Land, Operation, and Battleship.

61

DIFFERENT, BUT SAME

Welcome one another as Christ has welcomed you, for the glory of God.

ROMANS 15:7 ESV

WHEN GOD CREATED THE world, He filled it with colors. Different colors of plants, animals, and yes, people too. But whether it's the color of our skin, the clothes we wear, the way we talk, or where we're from, some will use the ways we are different to decide they don't like certain people. Or they'll say that some people are better than others. But what God says is what matters. And He says *all* people are created in His image (Genesis 1:27). And when it comes to being saved, those who believe in Jesus are *all* the same because we all belong to Him (Galatians 3:28).

Don't let differences make you afraid to reach out to someone in friendship and with the good news of Jesus. Be brave enough to look past what makes you different and look for the things that make you the same. Always remember this:

- No matter where a person is from, everyone needs a friend.
- No matter what language a person speaks, everyone needs kindness.
- No matter how someone looks on the outside, we all need Jesus on the inside.

We're all different in different ways. But in the most important way—the eternal way—we're all the same. We all need Jesus. So be brave and reach out to share the love of Jesus with everyone you can.

GET READY TO ROAR!

It's much easier to reach out to people from different countries when you know a little bit about that country. Pick a spot on the globe and then ask your parents to help you search the internet for more information about that place. What language do they speak? What sorts of plants and animals live there? What foods are popular there? Find a recipe—or a restaurant—and give one of those foods a try!

LORD, YOU CREATED EACH OF US TO BE SPECIAL AND UNIQUE IN OUR OWN WAY, AND YOU LOVE US ALL JUST THE SAME. HELP ME LOVE LIKE YOU. AMEN.

62

STOP, LOOK, AND LISTEN

"My sheep listen to my voice. I know them, and they follow me."

JOHN 10:27 ICB

GOD SPOKE TO MOSES through the burning bush (Exodus 3). He spoke through a blinding light to Saul (Acts 9). He even used a donkey to get a message through to a guy named Balaam (Numbers 22). So yeah, sometimes God gets His people's attention with something big and bold and wild. But more often, God speaks softly through the wonders of His creation, His people, and His Word. We just need to stop, look, and listen.

Have you ever hurried through your prayers, telling God everything you want Him to take care of and maybe tossing in a "thank You" or two before you say "amen"? I know I have. But how often do we stop to listen to what God wants to say to us? Do we even notice the answers He sends our way? We need to make time every day—several times a day—to stop, look, and listen for the voice of God.

Give it a try today. When a friend comes along to help just when you need it most, stop and thank God for that person He sent your way. Look at the wonders of His creation and "hear" how powerful He is as you listen to the sounds of nature. And when a verse pops into your thoughts (that's the Holy Spirit giving you a little help), listen to what God's Word is telling you.

God *is* speaking. So don't forget to stop, look, and listen.

DEAR GOD, HOW AMAZING IS IT THAT YOU WANT TO TALK TO ME? HELP ME NEVER TO BE TOO BUSY TO STOP, LOOK, AND LISTEN TO YOU. AMEN.

DID YOU KNOW?

Your ears are pretty amazing creations. God designed the shape of your ear to "catch" sound waves and pass them on to the inner ear. There, tiny hair cells convert the sound waves into nerve impulses and send them to your brain. And it's your brain that actually figures out the meaning of the sounds you hear. (Warning: If those hairs get damaged, they can't be fixed. So turn down the volume on those earbuds and headphones!)

63

THE ANCHOR

We have this hope as an anchor for the soul, sure and strong.

HEBREWS 6:19 ICB

ANCHORS COME IN ALL sizes and shapes. Some are hooked like a giant letter J; others are shaped like claws or spikes. Ancient anchors were often just big hunks of stone. Whatever their shape, anchors all have the same purpose: to hold a boat in place. When tossed overboard, an anchor keeps the boat from drifting away, especially in rough or stormy weather.

So why are we talking about anchors? Because even though you're not a boat, you need an anchor to keep you from drifting away from God. You see, here's how it works: We're like a boat floating along in this world. Waves of sin and storms of trouble rock our boat and threaten to pull us away from God. We need an anchor to keep us close to Him. Because God loves us so very much, that's exactly what He gives us: an anchor.

This anchor isn't made of metal or stone. It's not something you can see or pick up. Your anchor is God's own Son. Jesus came to earth and died on the cross for our sins. But that's only part of the story. Jesus was raised to life again and returned to heaven to be with His Father. And because He did all those things, when we tie ourselves to Him by believing and following Him, He anchors us to God.

How can you be sure you're tied to the anchor of Jesus? Love, follow, and hold tight to Him—and He won't let you drift away.

LORD, PLEASE HOLD TIGHT TO ME, AND HELP ME HOLD TIGHT TO YOU. AMEN.

DID YOU KNOW?

One of the world's largest anchors was built for the *Titanic* in 1912. It was 18 $\frac{1}{2}$ feet long and weighed over sixteen tons—or about the same as thirty polar bears! Some of the links in the anchor's chain were so huge that it took two men to carry just one link. But the record for largest anchor weighs in at seventy-five tons!

FIND THE ANCHORS!

We've hidden anchors throughout the illustrations in this book. Look through the pages and try to find them all! The answers are on page 192.

64

TAKE SOME TIME

"Be still and know that I am God."

PSALM 46:10 NCV

WE LIVE IN A world that's all about being busy. The busier we are, the more important we must be, right? Well, no. The truth is the busier we are . . . the busier we are.

You may be a kid, but you can get pretty busy too. You've got school, homework, and extra projects. You might also have one or two activities,

clubs, or sports. Then there's church and volunteering. You have friends to keep up with, Grandma's birthday party, and your cousin's dance recital. And don't forget all the everyday stuff like taking care of your pets, washing dishes, and brushing your teeth.

Life can get so busy that it's hard to breathe. You're going to need the courage to say no to a few things here or there. (Don't try that with chores, though. Trust me, that will *not* work out well.) Don't be busy just because everyone else is. Make sure the things that take up your time are things that honor God and are good for you. Give yourself time to stare up at the clouds, goof off, or take a nap once in a while. And every day, take some time to be still with God. Read His Word, pray, or simply sit with Him and be amazed that the God of the universe wants to hang out with you.

GET READY TO ROAR!

A "breath prayer" is a simple prayer that helps you slow down your racing mind and be still with God. First, close your eyes. Next, take a big, deep, slow breath in. As you breathe in, say God's name: *Father*, *Lord*, or *God*. Then, as you slowly breathe out all that air, say a truth about God, such as "I trust You" or "You are with me." Keep breathing and praying until you're filled with the peace of God. Now, doesn't that feel good?

DEAR GOD, PLEASE SHOW ME THE THINGS I SHOULD SAY YES TO AND THE THINGS I SHOULD SAY NO TO SO THAT I ALWAYS HAVE TIME FOR YOU. AMEN.

65

HIDE-AND-SEEK

**"You will search for me. And when you search for
me with all your heart, you will find me!"**

JEREMIAH 29:13 NCV

I LOVE GAMES. HIDE-AND-SEEK IS especially awesome. You pick out the perfect spot and then tuck yourself away to hide. Then there's the challenge to try to stay as still and quiet as possible—even when you can see the seeker's sneakers right outside your hiding place! Have you ever hidden so well that no one found you, and you won the whole game? That's really cool!

But it's also one thing God will never do. Don't get me wrong—God loves

fun and play and laughter. After all, He's the one who invented all that great stuff. But He *never* plays hide-and-seek. Why? Because God *wants* to be found.

Now, God probably won't swoop down out of heaven and introduce Himself with a "Hey, how are you?"—though He could if He wanted to. But He'll find a way to show Himself to you. It might be through the Bible or something else that you read. Or it might be through another person who helps you know God even better.

That's what He did for the Ethiopian man who was riding along in his chariot, reading through the Scriptures, and trying to learn about God. There was no one around to explain the scriptures to him, so God sent Philip to meet him. Philip explained what the scriptures meant, and the man believed and was saved! (Check out the full story in Acts 8:26–40.)

When you search for God, He'll always be found. Because God doesn't play hide-and-seek.

DID YOU KNOW?

People have been playing hide-and-seek for as far back as the second century. The rules are a little different from place to place. In some areas, hiders can try to run back to a home base to be safe from the seeker. In other places, each person who is found joins the seeker in looking for everyone else. Over the years, hide-and-seek has gone by other names, including *hide-and-go-seek*, *hide-and-find*, and the slightly strange *hide-and-coop*. Whatever you call it, grab some friends and enjoy a game of hide-and-seek today.

DEAR GOD, THANK YOU FOR NEVER HIDING FROM ME. I'M SO GLAD YOU WANT TO BE FOUND! AMEN.

66

EVERYWHERE YOU GO

Jesus went everywhere doing good.

ACTS 10:38 NCV

PEOPLE HAVE ALL KINDS of habits—things they do all the time without thinking much about them. Some people chew gum. Others always skip the last step and jump to the bottom instead. Some people even talk to their pets like they're people too. (Okay, that last one is about me. But I'm not alone, right? Right? Hello?)

We all have one habit or another. Even Jesus. What was His habit? Everywhere Jesus went, He did good.

In the Bible we read about a lot of really big good things that Jesus did—like healing the sick, helping the blind see, and even raising people from the dead. But Jesus didn't just go around doing huge, miraculous sorts of good things. A lot of the good He did was in the little, everyday moments of His life. Like talking to the Samaritan woman at the well—the woman nobody else really talked to—and telling her how to find God (John 4). Or like hugging a bunch of kids the disciples wanted to shoo away and telling them how important they were to Him (Matthew 19).

We may not be able to help the blind or heal the sick, but talking and hugging? Those are things we can do!

Did you make someone smile? Did you help someone feel welcome and included? Did you talk to someone about God? You can do something good everywhere you go. And that's a great habit to have!

GET READY TO ROAR!

———

Want to see how you can make a difference every day? Try this experiment: smile at every person you meet and notice how many people smile back. If a simple smile can do that, just imagine what else a little kindness and goodness can do! So try sharing a little goodness everywhere you go.

LORD, PLEASE SHOW ME THE GOOD I CAN DO IN THIS WORLD TODAY—AND THEN PLEASE SHOW ME THE WAY TO DO IT. AMEN.

67

LOOK FOR THE PEOPLE WHO CARE

"Be strong and courageous. Do not be afraid; do not be discouraged, for the LORD your God will be with you wherever you go."

JOSHUA 1:9 NIV

AS A KID, I was picked on *a lot*. I was kind of small, I had buckteeth, and I wore glasses. I tried playing sports so that I would fit in at school, but I also had asthma, which meant that I had trouble breathing sometimes, so the sports thing didn't work out too well for me. And let's just say the other kids were not very kind. Seriously. They made fun of me and called me names.

I tried my hardest to fit in with the cool kids by doing things they were doing—things I knew were wrong. But it didn't work anyway. Those kids still weren't my friends, and I was lonely. I kept feeling worse and worse until . . . I met a group of Christians who were way cooler than that crowd I was trying to fit in with. They were *nice* to me and actually wanted to get to know me. Those people gave me a glimpse of who God really is by the way they cared about me.

I'm telling you this because if you're being bullied, it can feel like the whole planet is against you. That's a lie straight from the devil. Stop worrying about fitting in with the cool crowd and look for people who really care. Search for the Christians who are living out what it means to love Jesus and let them show you God's love. Because—and I really want you to hear this—*you are worthy of being loved.*

HOLY FATHER, USE YOUR PEOPLE TO SHOW ME HOW GOOD YOU ARE. HELP ME FIND GOOD FRIENDS WHO REALLY CARE. AMEN.

DID YOU KNOW?

Did you know there are bullies in the Bible? You've probably heard of the giant Goliath, but he wasn't the only one. There was a group in the New Testament called the Pharisees. They were supposed to be in charge of teaching people about God, but what they really did was use their power as leaders to boss other people around. Have you ever gotten bossy? Maybe with a brother or sister or friend? Check out Philippians 2:3—it's the best "how not to be a bully" verse!

68

YOU'VE GOT TO DO SOMETHING

Defend the rights of the poor and suffering.

PSALM 82:3 ICB

THE SAME THING HAPPENS practically every day. Nick walks into the lunchroom, and you can see the fear on his face. He knows what's coming, and he doesn't have to wait long. "Here comes Nerdy Nick," the taunts start. A bully pushes in front of him in line. He bumps Nick's tray, spilling peas and sending his milk carton flying. Nick dodges a fake punch and makes it to his seat. He slumps down with a sigh of relief because he knows he got off easy today.

Sometimes you're not the one who's being bullied, but you are the one who sees it. Maybe it's not even in person, but it's in a group text or a comment in a video game or app. You're going to need some courage to stand up against it. Depending on just how big and mean and bully-ish the bully is, you might need *a lot* of courage.

Because you've got to do something. You can't sit there with your friends and watch Nick suffer day after day. That's not what you would want if it were happening to you, and that's not what Jesus would do. So if you can, stand up to the bully, and take some friends with you. If that's not a good idea—and sometimes it's not—get a grown-up involved, like a trusted teacher, principal, counselor, or parent. Either way, invite that kid who is being bullied into your circle of friends. Let the Nicks in your world know they don't have to face bullies alone and that Jesus is standing with them too.

LORD, GIVE ME THE COURAGE TO STAND UP FOR THOSE WHO CAN'T STAND UP FOR THEMSELVES. AMEN.

GET READY TO ROAR!

Be a noticer. That is, be someone who notices other people and welcomes them in. It's so easy to get caught up in talking to our circle of friends that we don't even see those who are standing off to the side. So decide today to be someone who notices the ones who are left out and bring them in. All it takes is a friendly smile and a wave. Open up your circle, and you just might make a new friend.

69

THROUGH THICK AND THIN

Never let loyalty and kindness leave you!

PROVERBS 3:3 NLT

LIKE BATMAN AND ROBIN, Woody and Buzz, or Elsa and Anna, the very best friends stick together through thick and thin—that means they'll stand by each other no matter what happens. Whether it's battling an evil villain, rescuing a friend, or saving a kingdom in trouble, friends help each other every chance they get. Another word for this is *loyalty*. And one of the most beautiful stories of loyalty is a true one. It's found in the Bible in the book of Ruth. But the story actually begins with Ruth's mother-in-law, Naomi.

Naomi and her family moved to the land of Moab, and her sons married

Moabite women. But when her husband and sons died, Naomi decided to return home to Bethlehem. She urged her daughters-in-law to go back to their own families. One did, but Ruth refused:

"Don't ask me to leave you! Don't beg me not to follow you! Every place you go, I will go. Every place you live, I will live. Your people will be my people. Your God will be my God. . . . I ask the Lord to punish me terribly if I do not keep this promise: Only death will separate us" (Ruth 1:16–17 ICB).

Ruth stood by Naomi no matter what happened. And God blessed Ruth for her loyalty. She even became the great-grandmother of King David and an ancestor of Jesus!

But Ruth's loyalty is nothing compared to the loyalty God shows to you. No matter what happens, whether good or bad, God is always there for you, always helping, always loving. He'll be right by your side every day—through thick and thin!

DID YOU KNOW?

In America, one way we show our loyalty to our country is with the Pledge of Allegiance. The pledge was written by Francis Bellamy back in 1892 in honor of the first celebration of Columbus Day, which would be a highlight of the Chicago World's Fair. Bellamy wanted every student in the country to recite the pledge together, and over 12 million did on October 12, 1892. Congress made Bellamy's words the official pledge in 1942. The words "under God" were added in 1954, and it hasn't been changed since.

GOD, THANK YOU FOR YOUR LOYALTY TO ME. TEACH ME HOW TO BE ALWAYS LOYAL TO YOU. AMEN.

70

STUCK

Fix your thoughts on what is true, and honorable, and right, and pure, and lovely, and admirable. Think about things that are excellent and worthy of praise.

PHILIPPIANS 4:8 NLT

STARTING IN LATE 2019, a crazy and terrible thing happened. A virus called COVID-19 invaded our world and began making some people sick. To keep the virus from spreading too much, everyone was told to stay at home as much as possible. Movie theaters, restaurants, and play-grounds were closed. Churches shut down. And instead of going to school, kids talked to their teachers and classmates and did their schoolwork on video calls from home. For a lot of that time, we were all stuck at home. And if we did go out, we wore a mask over our mouths and noses.

There were so many things we couldn't do. Even ordinary things, like go to a friend's house, visit grandparents, or head out to practice. And while it was so easy to focus on all the things we *couldn't* do, there were so many good and wonderful things we *could* do. Things like hanging out and playing games with our family, sleeping in, making phone calls to friends—and thanking God for having a home to be stuck in!

That's the trouble with trouble. It likes to steal your attention so that you only think about the trouble you're stuck in. There's a cure for that, though. Think about good things instead. It takes some work and some determination. But no matter how tough the day has been, you can always find something good to be thankful for. And when you do, you won't feel quite so *stuck* in your trouble.

DID YOU KNOW?

Have you ever seen a movie or cartoon where people get stuck in quicksand? The more they move, the deeper they get pulled in. You may have thought that only happens on TV, but quicksand is real! It's made of a mixture of sand and water. Because the water doesn't reach all the way to the top, quicksand looks just like regular sand. But if a person or animal steps on it, they'll begin to sink. If you ever find yourself stuck in quicksand, move slowly, spread out your arms and legs, and try to float on your back to safety.

LORD, WHEN I'M FEELING STUCK, SHOW ME ALL THE GOOD THINGS I HAVE TO BE THANKFUL FOR. AMEN.

71

EVERYTHING YOU NEED

Depend on the Lord. Trust him, and he will take care of you.

PSALM 37:5 ICB

IMAGINE STARING UP AT a rock-climbing wall. You've never climbed one before, and it's *really* tall. You're all the way down at the bottom, and the bell you're supposed to ring is all the way up at the top. The thought of climbing that high makes your tummy a little flip-floppy, but it also feels a little exciting. So you strap in, reach for the wall, and start to climb. It's a challenge, but you've just got to give it a try.

Challenges come along every day. Sometimes they're good challenges that give you the chance to do something new and exciting—like trying out for the school play, waterskiing, or reaching the top of a rock-climbing wall. Sometimes, though, challenges look more like troubles or obstacles—such as trying to figure out a difficult class in school, making new friends, or dealing with a family member's sickness.

Whatever challenge you face—whether it's good, not so good, or somewhere in between—here's one thing you can know for sure: God will take care of you. He'll give you everything you need in order to do what He wants you to do (Hebrews 13:20–21). He'll give you the courage to try something new and the determination to keep trying in a class that's hard. He'll give you the wisdom to choose good friends and a heart that tries to help those who are hurting.

God never leaves you to face a challenge on your own. So go ahead, be brave, and take on that challenge. Climb that wall!

GET READY TO ROAR!

People aren't the only ones God takes care of—He watches over all of His creation. Read Matthew 6:25–29, then head outside and take a good look around. How does God take care of the birds? How beautiful are the flowers that He gives such colorful "clothes" to? What's your favorite thing about the way God takes care of this world?

LORD, YOU KNOW EVERYTHING THAT I TRULY NEED—EVEN BEFORE I NEED IT. I TRUST YOU TO TAKE CARE OF ME. AMEN.

72

STRONGER THAN ANY STORM

God is our protection and our strength. He always helps in times of trouble. . . . We will not fear even if the oceans roar and foam, or if the mountains shake at the raging sea.

PSALM 46:1, 3 ICB

AT FIRST IT WAS just a raindrop or two. You saw the dark clouds and thought it was probably time to run inside. You dashed home, and once you got inside, you watched out the window. The rain fell so heavy and thick, you could hardly see a thing—except when the lightning flashed! Storms can be fierce and frightening. And you know what? It's okay to be scared. Just remember: Jesus is with you—and He's more powerful than any storm.

That's what the disciples learned long ago. You see, they were out in a boat on the lake. Jesus was with them, but He'd fallen asleep. Suddenly, a terrible storm came up. Now, the disciples were professional fishermen. They'd sailed through plenty of storms. But these waves were huge! And the wind felt like it was going to blow them overboard! Terrified, they hurried to wake up Jesus. They asked, "Don't you care if we drown?" (Mark 4:38 NIV). Of course Jesus cared! He just wasn't worried about the storm. Jesus told that storm to hush—and it did! Then he asked the disciples, "Why are you afraid?" (Matthew 8:26 ICB). Didn't they understand that the One who made the wind and waves was right there with them? They didn't have to be afraid.

And neither do you. If you're ever frightened by a storm, tell Jesus your fears. He might tell the storm to hush, or He might hush your fears. Either way, He'll be right there with you through it all.

FATHER, WHEN THE STORMS COME, I WILL TRUST YOU TO TAKE CARE OF ME. YOU ARE BIGGER THAN ANY STORM COULD EVER BE. AMEN.

73

DON'T HOLD BACK

Give yourselves completely to God.

JAMES 4:7 NCV

YOUR MOM ASKED YOU to clean up your room. So you do. *Sort of.* I mean, you make the bed, pick up everything off the floor, and clean off the desk. Except you stuff all the books, toys, clothes, and junk in the closet. Now your closet is so full, you can barely close it. There's even a candy bar wrapper and a shirt sleeve sticking out. When your mom walks in to check your room, she heads straight for the closet. Why? Because she knows what that closet door is holding back—a bunch of junk!

You can't fool moms, and you can't fool God either.

God asks you to give yourself completely to Him, and He knows when you're holding back on Him. He knows when you try to hide things. Like when you play that video game your parents don't know about. Or when you pretend to brush your teeth, but all you really do is stick your toothbrush under the faucet and get it wet. Or when you hang out with that friend who keeps pressuring you to do stuff you know you shouldn't do. Or when you don't tell God about that secret sin you're so ashamed of.

God knows all of it, but that's actually a good thing. God won't use those things you're holding back and hiding as a reason not to love, help, or save you. Instead, He'll use those things to show you how huge His love is, how willing He is to help you, and how much He wants to save you. Don't try to hide your mistakes from God. And don't hold anything back from Him. Because when God sent Jesus to save you, He didn't hold anything back from you.

DID YOU KNOW?

Beavers are masters of holding back—holding back water, that is! They use their sharp teeth to cut down trees. They then use those trees, along with sticks and mud, to build dams across creeks and streams. The dams hold back the water, changing the shape of the land and creating ponds where beavers can hide from predators like wolves, coyotes, bears, and eagles.

LORD, SHOW ME IF THERE ARE ANY PARTS OF MYSELF THAT I'M HOLDING BACK—AND HELP ME GIVE ALL OF ME TO YOU. AMEN.

74

PROOF IN CREATION

In the beginning God created the heavens and the earth.

GENESIS 1:1 NIV

ALBERT EINSTEIN WAS A brilliant scientist, but he also used to be a kid just like you. One day, when he was sick in bed, his dad gave him a gift. That gift changed his life. It was a compass, and it completely fascinated him. No matter how he shook it or which way he turned it, that little needle always found its way back to north. What was moving the needle? Einstein later said, "I can still remember—or at least believe I can remember—that this experience made a deep and lasting impression upon me. Something deeply hidden had to be behind things."

That hidden something was the magnetic fields of the earth—magnetic fields created by the power of God. He created the earth, the universe, *everything*. It's His power that set it all into motion—from the spinning of the stars to the falling of the rain to the very breath you pull into your lungs. And it's His love and care that keeps it all going (1 Corinthians 8:6). There are people in this world who have never read the Bible and who've never heard the truth of Jesus. But even they have to see a talented Maker behind every sunrise, wildflower, tree, and bird's feather. There is proof of God all over creation (Romans 1:20). All you have to do is look around at God's creation to know that He is real and He is amazing!

GET READY TO ROAR!

Grab a magnifying glass and go on a scavenger hunt through God's creation. Try to find as many of these things as you can: leaf, wildflower, insect, spider web, rock, blade of grass, bird feather, acorn, tree bark, seed, and pine cone. Examine each one with your magnifying glass. Notice all the details. What do you see? What else can you find? And what do your discoveries tell you about God?

LORD, AS I WALK THROUGH THIS DAY, OPEN MY EYES TO SEE ALL THE WONDERFUL PROOF THAT YOU ARE REALLY REAL AND THAT YOU ARE REALLY GOD. AMEN.

75

NOT-SO-COOL SCHOOLDAYS

The Lord said to me, "My grace is enough for you. When you are weak, then my power is made perfect in you."

2 CORINTHIANS 12:9 ICB

YOU'RE SITTING AT YOUR school desk, staring at the test. The only sounds in the room are the scratching of pencils and the teacher shuffling her papers. Everyone else is working away, but you have no idea how to even get started. The words on the page are just a jumble. You have no idea what to do, and you can already tell this is going to be yet another bad grade.

Has this ever happened to you? For some, school is a breeze, but for others, school is a nightmare. Maybe you feel this way because you never can seem to figure out how to do the work. Maybe it's just in reading or math or science, or maybe it's all the subjects. You listen. You pay attention. But there are some things you just can't seem to figure out.

Or maybe it's not the schoolwork. Maybe it's a tough teacher, a difficult classmate, or a lack of friends. Whatever the reason, school can be hard sometimes. And it can make you feel trapped because you still have to go every day.

But you don't have to go alone. God is with you, and He promises to give you the strength you need to keep going. Does that mean He'll give you the answers to that big test? No. But it does mean that He'll help you remember you're so much more important than any number or grade or popularity test. And no matter what your report card says, you're a star student to Him.

DID YOU KNOW?

The very first public school opened in the United States before there ever was a United States. The Boston Latin School opened on April 23, 1635, in Boston, Massachusetts. Students learned Latin, Greek, and a handful of other subjects. John Hancock (who had the biggest signature on the Declaration of Independence) went to Boston Latin, and so did Benjamin Franklin—but he dropped out! (By the way, most Ivy League colleges in America—including Princeton, Harvard, and Yale— were founded by the church.)

LORD, WHEN SCHOOL IS TOUGH, SHOW ME THAT I'M SO MUCH MORE IMPORTANT TO YOU THAN ANY NUMBER OR GRADE. AMEN.

76

BE A
BARNABAS

Encourage one another and build each other up.

1 THESSALONIANS 5:11 NIV

IMAGINE THIS: YOU AND your best friend both try out for the basketball team—and you both make it! For the next week, all you can talk about is the fun you'll have together. But the day before the first practice, your friend stumbles and twists an ankle. She can't play again for weeks and has to use crutches. She's upset, sad, and disappointed. What do you do?

Here's the thing: Life is tough sometimes. We all have bad days and sad days. And just as you need people to encourage you, other people—like that friend—need encouragement too.

There's a guy in the Bible named Barnabas. Actually, his name was Joseph, but the disciples nicknamed him Barnabas, which means "one who encourages" (Acts 4:36 ICB). Isn't that the best nickname? Imagine being so good at building up others that all your friends start calling you "The Encourager." Now, sure, Barnabas did some big things—like preaching about Jesus to big crowds. But he also helped new believers fit in with the church, and he was willing to give a second chance to friends who had messed up. It was these little things of encouragement that Barnabas was best known for. Maybe that's because encouragement isn't a little thing at all. It's huge, especially to the one who's being encouraged.

So how could you encourage your injured friend? Maybe you could help her study the team's playbook, or you could chase down the ball for her while she practices her shots. What can you do for the people around you today? Be creative. Be encouraging. Be a Barnabas!

GET READY TO ROAR!

What are you really good at? Is it singing, drawing, planting flowers, baking, or building things? Is it listening or writing notes? Write down three things you are really good at. Next to each one, write a way you can use that gift to encourage someone else. Maybe you can teach praise songs to younger kids, bake cookies for a neighbor, help a younger friend learn to ride a skateboard, or send a note to a friend who's having a tough day. It doesn't have to be big— just show that you care.

LORD, SHOW ME WHO I CAN ENCOURAGE AND HOW I CAN BE AN ENCOURAGEMENT TODAY. AMEN.

WARNING! WARNING!

The Holy Spirit warns me.

IN ENGLAND, IN 1902, George Andrew Darby invented one of the first fire alarms. Tucked inside the alarm was a block of butter—yes, butter! If temperatures got hot enough to melt the butter, it would trigger the alarm. Unfortunately, the alarm was so big and bulky that it could only be used in larger buildings. It wasn't until 1955 that an alarm was made for homes, but it was so expensive most people couldn't afford it. Thankfully, these days, most homes have some sort of fire and smoke alarm. Alarms warn us of danger and give us time to get to safety.

And that's also what the Holy Spirit does. He warns you of sin and other dangers so you can get to safety. The Holy Spirit is the Spirit of God who comes to live inside you when you decide to follow Jesus. He teaches, guides, and helps you remember God's Word (John 14:26). *And* He warns you of danger. His warning probably won't be big and blaring like a fire alarm. Instead, He might pop a verse into your thoughts to remind you to do what's right. He might use a friend to warn you about not doing something or going somewhere. Or He might "nudge" your heart to tell you something isn't right. But the Holy Spirit never, ever disagrees with God's Word. So watch and listen for His warnings, and let Him help you stay away from danger.

DEAR GOD, PLEASE HELP ME TO HEAR AND FOLLOW THE WARNINGS OF YOUR HOLY SPIRIT. AMEN.

GET READY TO ROAR!

Hopefully you'll never have a house fire, but it's good to have an escape plan in place. Ask your parents to help you. First, find two ways to escape from every room. Make sure doors and windows are easy to open. You might need a collapsible ladder for upper floors. (If you live in an apartment, never get in an elevator if there's a fire.) And pick a spot outside for everyone to meet. Next, practice your plan. Most important of all, make sure there are working alarms on every level of your house—so you have plenty of warning!

78

LEAD THE WAY!

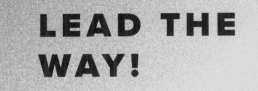

Be an example to show the believers how they should live. Show them with your words, with the way you live, with your love, with your faith, and with your pure life.

1 TIMOTHY 4:12 ICB

YOU ARE A leader—it's true. Now, you may be thinking, *Nope. That's not me. I'm the one who sits in the back row every chance I get. I'm the one who stares at the floor when the teacher asks for a volunteer. No, I'm definitely not a leader.*

But you are. Because everyone is. No matter how old you are, how quiet you are, or how far you slink down behind your desk to hide, someone is watching to see what you do. It might be someone in your class. It might be a brother, a sister, a neighbor, or a little kid who is younger than you. But someone is always watching. And that's why you need to be careful about how and where you lead them.

Does that mean you have to jump up in front of everyone and start telling people what to do? No! In fact, that would be a pretty bad idea. But you should try to set a good example for whoever might be watching you. Make sure the words you say are kind and helpful and true. Help others whenever you can—in big ways or in simple, everyday ways. Leadership isn't about having a fancy title or being in charge. It's about being a good example. Show the world how much you love God by showing love to those around you. And then you'll be leading the way!

GET READY TO ROAR!

Grab some friends and play a game of follow-the-leader. Choose one person as the leader. Everyone else lines up behind them. The leader then begins moving around—jumping, skipping, spinning in a circle, quacking like a duck, whatever they want to do. Everyone else must copy what the leader does. Whoever doesn't is out. The last person left becomes the new leader. As you play, remember that people are watching how you lead.

GOD, HELP ME BE A GOOD EXAMPLE AND LEADER TO WHOEVER MIGHT BE WATCHING ME. AMEN.

79

A GOOD PLAN

"I have good plans for you. I don't plan to hurt you. I plan to give you hope and a good future."

JEREMIAH 29:11 ICB

PRETEND YOU'RE RIDING A roller coaster for the very first time. You're slowly climbing up a huge hill, and you know that at the top you're going to zoom right down again. But what will happen after that? Will there be a big turn? Will you flip upside down? Will there be another hill? You'll just have to wait and see.

God's plans for you can be a bit like that roller coaster. Big, huge, exciting, and sometimes unexpected. Because God won't tell you every detail of His plans—only the next step or two. Just like on that roller coaster, you'll have wait to find out what comes next.

Another thing you need to know about God's plans is that they are huge and so very important to Him and His kingdom. And they might look huge and so very important to the world—like leading a church, becoming a missionary, or writing a book about God. *Or* they might look like taking care of a friend, cleaning up a classroom, or using puppets to tell a Bible story. The world might call those things small, but to God, they're huge!

God has plans for you, and they're always good plans. Knowing that can give you the courage to keep following Him, especially when His plans don't make sense. Trust God, and He'll work everything out for your good.

DEAR GOD, I BELIEVE YOU HAVE A GOOD PLAN FOR MY LIFE. PLEASE GIVE ME THE COURAGE TO FOLLOW IT EVEN WHEN I DON'T UNDERSTAND IT. AMEN.

DID YOU KNOW?

God is the one who controls the plans for our lives, and sometimes He uses our lives to help others. Or, as with Mother Teresa, to help *thousands and thousands* of others. Mother Teresa was only twelve when she knew she wanted to help the poor. She became a nun and dedicated her life to helping the poorest of the poor in India. She set up shelters, helped lepers, and opened a home for orphans. God used her to not only help others but to show the world that every person—no matter how sick or poor or lost—is precious to Him.

80

CRAZY FEAR

I asked the Lord for help, and he answered
me. He saved me from all that I feared.

PSALM 34:4 ICB

 OME FEARS ARE PERFECTLY logical. For example, if you take a step outside and see a giant, growling grizzly bear charging down the street and headed straight for you, it makes sense to be afraid. You might wonder how this huge, hairy beast happened to be on your street, but being afraid of it would be perfectly reasonable.

Other fears aren't so logical. Like me and spiders. I hate those guys. In my head, I know I'm like a zillion times bigger than they are. I could squish one with my little toe—covered in a massive steel-toed boot, of course. But when I see a spider, all I can think about are those eight creepy little legs crawling up my arm. I know my fear is crazy, but if I see a spider, I'm outta here. And don't get me started on snakes!

Maybe you have a crazy fear too. Maybe it's a fear of numbers—which, by the way, is called *arithmophobia*. Or maybe it's just the number eight—*octophobia*. Maybe you're afraid of heights or speaking in front of people. Just because your fear seems crazy doesn't mean you aren't afraid.

But don't let fear keep you from experiencing everything God has planned for you. Sure, there may be spiders in that cabin, but I'm not missing that camping trip. Don't you miss out either—on riding the tallest roller-coaster ride, telling people about Jesus, or even visiting the octopus exhibit at the zoo. Give your fears—crazy or not—to God, and He'll help you be brave.

DID YOU KNOW?

Some people aren't just reasonably scared of bears; they are terrified of all kinds of bears. This fear is called *arkoudaphobia*. I have no idea how to pronounce it, but I do know it means a fear of all kinds of bears—whether they're angry grizzly bears, wandering black bears, or cute and cuddly panda bears. It even describes people who are afraid of teddy bears!

LORD, I DON'T WANT MY FEARS—REAL OR CRAZY—TO KEEP ME FROM ALL YOU HAVE PLANNED FOR ME. I WILL TRUST YOU TO HELP ME BE BRAVE. AMEN.

81

REACH OUT

Do not be interested only in your own life, but
be interested in the lives of others.

PHILIPPIANS 2:4 ICB

I F YOU'RE LIKE ME, you can see problems all around you. You want to help, but you end up thinking something like this:

I see the homeless people in my city, but it's such a huge problem— how can I help? I see that kid who gets pushed around at school, but I am afraid those mean kids will turn on me if I say anything. What if I just make things worse for myself? My Sunday school teacher wants me to be part of a skit for the whole church, but what if I mess it up? I want to be brave and do good things, but . . . I am scared.

Look at that last paragraph again. Count how many times the word *I*, *me*, *my*, or *myself* pops up. *Fourteen.* Fourteen times in just one paragraph. That's the real reason we aren't being brave as often as we could and should be—we're thinking and worrying too much about ourselves. There's a fix for that, though. Change your thoughts from *I* and *me* to *others* and how you can reach out to help them.

In other words, you don't have to help every homeless person on the planet. Just smile and offer a bottle of water to one. You don't have to take on all the mean kids at school. Just invite that pushed-around kid to sit with you. And that skit doesn't have to win an Academy Award, so stop worrying and help tell the story. Because one of the best ways to be brave is to reach out and help someone else.

GET READY TO ROAR!

It's time for something I like to call Operation Reach Out! Make a list of all the things you can do to reach out to others. You could include things like collect socks and mittens for the homeless, write a note to someone in a nursing home, invite the new kid from school to come over and play, or do an extra chore for your parents. Once the list is finished, get up and reach out!

LORD, HELP ME TO THINK LESS ABOUT MYSELF AND MORE ABOUT OTHERS. AMEN.

82

EYES ON THE SON

Jesus immediately reached out and grabbed him.

MATTHEW 14:31 NLT

MATTHEW 14:31 IS ONE of my all-time favorite verses, and it's all because of one little word—*immediately*. This verse pops up near the end of Peter's quick little stroll across the water. Have you heard that story? It's amazing! Let me tell you what happened.

God's Son, Jesus, sent the disciples in the boat to cross the lake while He went to the top of a hill to have a nice, peaceful talk with God. The disciples, however, didn't have such a peaceful time. A huge wind blew, knocking the boat, and waves crashed against them. Then, they spotted someone walking to them *on the water*. They were terrified. (Who wouldn't be?) But Jesus said, "It is I" (Matthew 14:27 NCV). Peter called back, "If it is really you, then command me to come to you on the water" (v. 28 NCV). Jesus did, and Peter stepped out of that boat and *walked on the water*. But somewhere between the boat and the Son of God, Peter took his eyes off Jesus and saw the wind and waves instead. And he began to sink. "Lord, save me!" Peter shouted (v. 30 NCV). *Immediately* Jesus reached out and caught Peter.

Did you get that? *Immediately*. Jesus didn't scold. He didn't stop to think about whether Peter was "worth" saving. Jesus immediately reached out and caught Peter. Why is that my favorite part? Because we all take our eyes off the Son of God sometimes. When we start to sink, all we have to do is call out, and Jesus will immediately reach out and catch us. *He'll catch you.*

LORD, THANK YOU FOR ALWAYS BEING READY AND WILLING TO CATCH ME AND SAVE ME. AMEN.

DID YOU KNOW?

Bucephalus was the horse of Alexander the Great. (Alexander was this famous military leader from before Jesus was born.) Bucephalus was a huge, magnificent black stallion, but nobody could ride him. That is, until Alexander came along and turned the horse to face the sun. You see, Alexander realized that Bucephalus was afraid of his own shadow. When Alexander fixed the horse's eyes on the sun, he couldn't see the thing that scared him. That's kind of like us when we fix our eyes on Jesus, the Son of God. When we're looking at Him, we won't focus on our fears.

83

IT'S OKAY TO NOT BE OKAY

Jesus wept.

JOHN 11:35 NIV

IT'S OKAY TO NOT be okay. It's okay to hurt, to cry, and to be angry. It's okay to feel all the yucky things. Because you know what? Everybody goes through hard times. And not every day is going to be full of bike rides through the sunshine. Bad, sad, and hurtful things happen. It takes courage to admit you're struggling and to not just pretend everything is all right.

You can't stay there, though. You can't put up a tent in the middle of those yucky feelings and just camp out for the rest of your life. You have to decide what you're going to do next, and do it. And the best thing to do is give all those yucky feelings to Jesus. Now, maybe you're thinking, *I don't want to dump all these ugly thoughts on Jesus. He's so good and perfect—what if He doesn't understand?* But that's a big part of the reason Jesus came to earth in the first place. So He would understand everything you're going through.

Jesus cried. He got angry. He was betrayed and hurt. Because Jesus went through all those things Himself, He knows exactly how to help you. He'll comfort and guide you and help you do what you need to do—whether it's forgive someone, move on, or dust yourself off and try again.

So yeah, it's okay to not be okay. But don't keep it to yourself. Talk to Jesus. Because it's also okay to feel okay again.

GET READY TO ROAR!

After Jesus wept, He went to help His friends (John 11:17–44). When He was angry because the money changers were cheating God's people, He stood up for what was right (Mark 11:15–17). And even when He knew He was going to be betrayed and hurt, He still did what God wanted Him to do (John 13). When you're feeling all the yucky feelings, remember what Jesus did and try to do the same: help someone, stand up for what is right, and do what you know God wants you to do.

LORD, I'M SO THANKFUL I CAN SHARE EVEN MY WORST THOUGHTS AND FEELINGS WITH YOU. I KNOW YOU'LL HELP ME BE OKAY AGAIN. AMEN.

84

TURN IT AROUND

I will instruct you and teach you in the way you should go.

PSALM 32:8 NIV

DO YOU EVER HAVE a day when everything seems to go wrong? The alarm clock doesn't go off, so you're running late. In your rush to brush your teeth, a big glop of toothpaste dribbles all down your shirt. The back of your hair is sticking up like some kind of weird bird tail. Could this day get any worse? Yep. Because when you grab your backpack, everything spills out, and you discover that the dog *really did* eat your homework. Then it's hurry, hurry out the door . . . just in time to see the school bus pull away. Wow! What a horrible day! And it's just getting started.

Here's where you have a choice to make: Are you going mope, whine, and complain and let the rest of this day slide downhill because you've had a tough morning? Or are you going to take a deep breath, be strong, and turn this thing around?

Don't let one bad morning ruin your whole day. For that matter, don't let one bad *anything* ruin your whole day. Turn it around. Sure, your morning just blew up, but God is still good and He's still pouring His goodness into your life. Ask Him to help you see it. Then figure out something good you can do for someone else and do it. That's one of the best ways to turn a bad day around.

LORD, WHEN IT SEEMS LIKE EVERYTHING IS GOING WRONG, SHOW ME ALL THE THINGS THAT ARE GOING RIGHT. AMEN.

DID YOU KNOW?

Some people think Friday the 13th is doomed to be a bad day. There's even a name for that fear—*paraskevidekatriaphobia*. (I'm not even going to try to pronounce that one!) Other people think the number thirteen is unlucky, but that's just a superstition. In fact, for bakers in England, way back in the 1200s, thirteen was a lucky number. You see, if their dozen loaves of bread baked a little small, they could be accused of cheating their customers! To be safe, bakers gave customers thirteen loaves—a baker's dozen.

85

PRAYING BRAVE

Let us come boldly to the throne of our gracious God.

HEBREWS 4:16 NLT

WHEN YOU THINK ABOUT bravery in the Bible, who do you think of? Abraham leaving everything to follow God? Shadrach, Meshach, and Abednego facing the fiery furnace? Or maybe it's Deborah the judge heading off into battle. But does Hannah ever pop into your mind?

Hannah? Isn't she the lady who prayed for a baby? What's so brave about that? Hannah's bravery was in the way she poured out her heart's dream to God *completely*—so completely that tears streamed from her eyes. Hannah trusted God with her heart's deepest longings, and God blessed her.

Do you ever have trouble asking God for your heart's dream? Does it maybe feel a little bit selfish? God wants you to come to Him with *everything*, not just the things you need and not just prayers for others. Ask Him for the things you hope and dream for. Then pray as Jesus did: "I want your will to be done, not mine" (Mark 14:36 NLT). That means you're willing to accept God's answer and to praise Him no matter what, even if you don't get the thing you want. Whether His answer is no, yes, or not right now, He has wonderful things ahead for you!

GOD, I WANT TO TELL YOU ALL MY HOPES AND DREAMS. AMEN.

DID YOU KNOW?

If you ever meet a member of Britain's royal family, there are a few rules you need to know. When you first meet, curtsy or bow your head. Never shake hands unless they offer first. Be early—a royal should never have to wait for you. Don't sit or eat until after they do. And *never, ever* speak unless you are spoken to first. Whew! And that's only some of the rules! But you don't have to worry about any rules when it comes to talking to the King of all creation. Because Jesus came and made a way for us to talk to God, you can talk to Him anytime, anywhere, and about anything!

86

NEVER TOO TIRED

The people who trust the LORD will become strong again.
They will rise up as an eagle in the sky; they will run and
not need rest; they will walk and not become tired.

ISAIAH 40:31 NCV

DO YOU GET TIRED? Do you ever just want to crawl back in bed and pull the covers up over your head? I sure do. And I'll let you in on a secret: sometimes I get tired of trying to do the good things I know God wants me to do. Does that happen to you?

Because not everyone says "thank you" when you help them. Some people even get upset when you do what's right. (Like when you refuse to let a classmate copy your homework answers, and he blames you when he gets a bad grade. What's up with that?) And then sometimes it seems as if no one notices the good things you do anyway, so why bother?

Why? Because your heavenly Father *always* notices. He sees the things you do for others, even the things you do in secret (Matthew 6:1–4). And He gives you a promise: trust Him when you're tired, and He'll make you strong again—as strong as an eagle soaring through the skies. Never get so tired that you stop doing good (Galatians 6:9). Let God fill your heart with the love, energy, and courage you need to show the world how wonderful He is.

LORD, WHEN I'M TIRED, HELP ME REMEMBER WHY I DO GOOD THINGS. IT'S NOT FOR MYSELF—IT'S TO HELP OTHERS SEE YOU. AMEN.

DID YOU KNOW?

The bald eagle is the national symbol of the United States. You'll find the bald eagle's image in statues, on buildings, and even on our money. In fact, the eagle printed on US money was modeled after a real-life eagle named Peter who often visited the first US Mint in Philadelphia back in the 1830s. Peter loved to sit on the machinery and watch the workers. And the workers loved him too— soon Peter had access to every vault in the Mint!

87

SEEING GOD

No one has seen God, but Jesus is exactly like him.

COLOSSIANS 1:15 ICB

WANT TO KNOW WHAT God looks like? Does He have brown eyes or a fluffy white beard? Well, there's no way to know exactly what God looks like on the outside—at least not until we see Him in heaven one day. But we can know what His heart looks like. How? By looking at Jesus and the way He lived when He was here on earth. You see, the Bible tells us that Jesus is exactly like God. So anyone who has seen Jesus has seen God (John 14:9). And you can see Jesus anytime you want—in the Bible.

Do you see Jesus? He's the guy who

- talked to people nobody else would talk to (John 4:1–42);
- welcomed children with a great big hug (Matthew 19:13–15);
- celebrated and cried with friends (John 2:1–11; John 11:35);
- forgave His friend when he messed up (John 21:15–17);
- helped those around Him to be the best that they could be (Matthew 5–7);
- did good whenever He could (Acts 10:38); and
- loved others even more than Himself (John 3:16).

That's who Jesus is. And because we've seen Him in the Bible, we can know that's who God is too. That's important because following God isn't always the easiest thing. It takes some courage. So we need to know that the God we're following is a good God. And He is! Just look—He's the One doing all the good.

DID YOU KNOW?

What do you see when you look in the mirror? An image of yourself, of course. But did you know that we don't start recognizing ourselves in the mirror until we're about eighteen months old? People are one of the few members of God's creation who know their own reflections. Others include monkeys and apes, dolphins, orcas, and elephants. But the real question is this: Do others see the image of Jesus in you?

LORD, I HAVE SO MANY REASONS TO THANK YOU FOR SENDING JESUS. AND ONE OF THEM IS SO I CAN SEE YOU. THANK YOU! AMEN.

88

NOTHING IS WASTED

**We know that in everything God works for
the good of those who love him.**

ROMANS 8:28 NCV

WHEN YOU LOVE AND follow God, He uses everything in your life to make your faith stronger. He uses good things, like loving parents, to show you how He loves you. He uses everyday things, like the sunset, to show you that He's always there. He uses big things, like the stars, to show His might and power. And He uses little things, like the colors of a flower petal, to show how He cares about all the details of your life. With God, nothing is ever wasted, not even your struggles. God uses your struggles to make you stronger.

How can struggles make you stronger? Think about a butterfly. If you watch a new butterfly struggling to escape from its cocoon, you might be tempted to help it. Yet it's actually important for that butterfly to struggle. As it fights to escape the cocoon, the butterfly exercises its wing muscles and makes them stronger. Without that fight, its wings would be too weak for flying. In other words, it must fight before it can fly.

Are you in a "fight" right now? Trust God to use that struggle to make you stronger. For example, if you're struggling because your best friend moved to a different school, God can use this time to teach you that He's the very best friend you could ever have. And because you've struggled with friendships, you'll understand what a difference you can make when you reach out to someone who needs a friend.

Whatever your struggle is, talk to God about it. Trust that He won't waste this tough time in your life. And look for the ways your struggle is making you stronger.

DID YOU KNOW?

There's more to butterflies than just their pretty wings. While most butterflies flutter along at about five to twelve miles per hour, the skipper butterfly zooms by at speeds of up to thirty-seven miles per hour. But there's no flying for any butterfly on cold days. That's because butterflies are cold-blooded—yes, like snakes! That means they need to soak up the warmth of the sun before they can fly.

HOLY FATHER, I KNOW YOU WON'T LET MY STRUGGLES GO TO WASTE. PLEASE USE THEM TO MAKE MY FAITH STRONGER. AMEN.

89

THE WAY IT'S SUPPOSED TO BE

"Look! I am making everything new!"

REVELATION 21:5 ICB

N THE THIRD CHAPTER of Genesis, we learn about "the fall." That's when Adam and Eve took a big ol' bite of the one fruit God said not to eat. And that's also when every kind of sin and sad and bad thing came into the world. Adam and Eve had to leave the garden of Eden, and we've struggled with sin ever since.

Here's something you may not have thought about before: people weren't the only ones to fall. You see, in the beginning, God made everything

good (Genesis 1:31), but sin changed *everything*. Nothing was the way it was supposed to be anymore. The whole world fell, and the whole world is groaning (Romans 8:22). Every squirrel, stream, sunset, and seahorse is bucking and bellowing, twisting and moaning, because things aren't the way they're supposed to be. Thorns, tornados, venom, cancer, and war—none of that was supposed to be a part of God's creation.

And one day, they won't be. One day, Jesus will come again. Satan will be tossed out (Revelation 20:10), and there will be a new heaven and a new earth (2 Peter 3:10, 13). And everything will be exactly the way God designed it to be. There will be no sin, no sorrow, no sickness or sadness. There will be peace and joy and love and beauty greater than anything we can imagine. Best of all, there will be God—and we will be with Him forever.

GET READY TO ROAR!

God gave the apostle John a glimpse of heaven, and he wrote all that he saw. Check it out for yourself in Revelation 21:1–4, 9–27. Just imagine all the things you'll never need again when God's creation is back to the way it's supposed to be. Things like hospitals, bandages, and tissues for tears. What are some other things you won't need in heaven? There is one thing you might need, though—some extra shades, because the glory of God is always shining!

HOLY FATHER, THANK YOU FOR SENDING JESUS SO THAT ONE DAY I CAN SEE YOUR CREATION THE WAY IT WAS MADE TO BE. AMEN.

90

YOUR ROAR STORY

You have good news to tell. Shout out loud the good news. Shout it out and don't be afraid.

ISAIAH 40:9 ICB

DO YOU HAVE A favorite story? Maybe it's about a guy with a really cool flying suit that made you want to be an astronaut. Or a super-smart detective who made you want to solve mysteries. Or maybe it's about a woman who spent her life helping the poor and inspired you to be a helper too. Stories make us laugh, cry, wonder, and dream. They teach us, guide us, and help us do brave things. And the best stories are the ones written by God.

God writes His stories with the lives of the people who love and follow Him—and the Bible is filled with their stories. There's Abraham and Sarah, Esther, Peter, John, and so many more. God used their lives and even their struggles to tell the world about His great love.

God's writing the story of your life too. Long before you were born, He planned how the story would go. He knows every twist and turn in the plot, and He's got a plan to work out each one (Psalm 139:16). Best of all, He knows how He wants the story to end—with you in heaven with Him.

But you have to let God have the pen. Don't snatch up the pen and pretend you're in control of your life and can write your own story. Only God has that kind of control. He wants the story of your life to roar through this world—to be an epic adventure, one that will thrill you and help others find Him. All you have to do is be brave enough to let go of the pen.

DID YOU KNOW?

A lion's roar is loud. *Really loud.* It can be heard up to five miles away! Scientists have measured a lion's roar at 114 decibels—making it about twenty-five times louder than a lawn mower. While most animals have triangle-shaped vocal cords, God shaped the lion's vocal cords like a square, and that's what makes their roars so loud. Trust God to shape your roar story—and see how far away you'll be heard.

LORD, I GIVE YOU THE PEN. WRITE MY STORY, AND LET IT ROAR WITH THE GOOD NEWS OF HOW WONDERFUL YOU ARE. AMEN.

ABOUT THE AUTHOR

LEVI LUSKO is the founder and lead pastor of Fresh Life Church located in Montana, Wyoming, Oregon, and Utah, as well as online. He is the best-selling author of *Through the Eyes of a Lion*, *Swipe Right*, and *I Declare War*. When Levi was a little boy, he loved playing tennis, riding in Jeeps, being in the mountains, and going to church, and he still loves those things today. He and his wife, Jennie, have one son, Lennox, and four daughters: Alivia, Daisy, Clover, and Lenya, who is in heaven.

ABOUT THE ILLUSTRATOR

CATHERINE PEARSON is a Swiss illustrator based in the hills of Lausanne, Switzerland. With a European bachelor's degree in illustration, Catherine has refined a unique and playful illustration style. She is passionate about bringing clients' ideas to life and believes illustration can speak to you where words cannot. Her sharp eye for color and composition brings a unique and striking originality.

HOW MANY ANCHORS DID YOU FIND?

OATS HAVE ANCHORS TO keep them from drifting away in the water. To keep us from drifting away in the trials and temptation of this world, God gave us an anchor to keep us close to Him. That anchor is Jesus. So every time my family sees an anchor, we think about how much God loves us and keeps us connected to heaven through His Spirit who lives in us. He loves us so much that He sent His Son, Jesus, to save us. Now, whenever you see an anchor, I hope you'll remember how much God loves you too!

To help you remember that Jesus anchors us to God, there are twenty anchors hidden throughout the illustrations in this book (including the not-so-hidden one on this page). How many did you find? Here's where they're hidden: pages 3, 12, 16, 20, 36, 40, 44, 52, 74, 78, 84, 88, 102, 104, 116, 134, 150, 166, 192.